Bigger Penis

Powerful and Realistic Methods on How to Supersize your Penis and Reverse the Most Common Male Issues Such as Erectile Dysfunction, Premature Ejaculation, Low Libido, and More!

Alec McKinney

This document is geared towards providing exact and reliable information in regards to the topic and issue covered. The publication is sold with the idea that the publisher is not required to render accounting, officially permitted, or otherwise, qualified services. If advice is necessary, legal or professional, a practiced individual in the profession should be ordered.

- From a Declaration of Principles which was accepted and approved equally by a Committee of the American Bar Association and a Committee of Publishers and Associations.

The information provided herein is stated to be truthful and consistent, in that any liability, in terms of inattention or otherwise, by any usage or abuse of any policies, processes, or directions contained within is the solitary and utter responsibility of the recipient reader. Under no circumstances will any legal responsibility or blame be held against the publisher for any reparation, damages, or monetary loss due to the information herein, either directly or indirectly.

Respective authors own all copyrights not held by the publisher.

The information herein is offered for informational purposes solely, and is universal as so. The presentation of the information is without contract or any type of guarantee assurance.

The trademarks that are used are without any consent, and the publication of the trademark is without permission or backing by the trademark owner. All trademarks and brands within this book are for clarifying purposes only and are the owned by the owners themselves, not affiliated with this document.

TABLE OF CONTENTS

INTRODUCTION

Have you ever felt that your confidence in bed is lacking, because of what your partner might think about your penis size? Have you ever wished that you had a thicker or longer penis and wondered what benefits it might have on your sex life? If you answered yes to any of these questions, then congratulations for taking a crucial step towards becoming more confident, not only inside the bedroom but in many other areas of your life.

A lot of men believe that the topic of penis size is taboo. That you are pretty much stuck with what your genes gave you.

The positive psychological, physiological, and emotional effects of having a more impressive male organ have in the life of men can be pretty profound. Another added benefit is that your lover or partner will also appreciate these welcome changes.

Let's start by mentioning the obvious: the information included inside this guide is no magic pill that will make your penis grow 3 inches in a week. Let's leave that to the scam ads seen often on the internet. However, with some consistency, the advice and strategies that you'll read in these pages will help you see substantial gains in both girth and length.

The fact that there is no magic substance that will boost penis growth is good news. If there indeed were a way to grow your penis 3 inches in a single week, then a lot of men would have penises that are significantly above average. What would be so special about having a large penis then?

However, since the information in this guide remains mostly unknown, those that have it will have a powerful tool at their disposal — one that can not only change their enjoyment of sex but of life as a whole. You might think this is an exaggeration, but we only need to see the suffering of men with small penis syndrome to understand.

As with anything regarding health, results will vary from individual to individual. However, most men that stick to the plan for some time can realistically see results after a few weeks.

Most men are aware that the penis enlargement industry is full of frauds, scammers, misinformation, and dangerous procedures that can have irreversible health side effects. Men from most cultures want to be part of the select few that have been blessed genetically with a big penis.

A lot of men have been bombarded by scam e-mails throughout their lives, with products that promise to add several inches to their penis by popping a pill every day. There is no end to the number of people wanting to prey on men that have always wanted some extra size below the belt.

Then there's another route: surgery. Men who are desperate for some extra size have probably heard that the only option is to undergo a risky surgery that might have dangerous side effects.

Because of the above, most men and women firmly believe that male enhancement is a myth, or that the only option available is a risky medical procedure. Getting to the real information in the world of male enhancement can be extremely tricky due to all the false claims, knowledge, and beliefs.

I wrote this guide for a few different purposes: to give you different options that will help you get closer to the penis size you always wanted and to provide you with the knowledge that will help you cure or significantly improve some of the most common male sexual health issues. Everything from erectile dysfunction and low libido to ejaculation size will be covered.

The great news is that you can start applying the advice and techniques today to start seeing some benefit as soon as possible. Also, all of the information included in the book is very safe and will be no threat to your health when practiced correctly.

I highly recommend reading this guide right from the beginning, before you decide to start on any male enhancement routine.

Thanks for reading. I hope you enjoy your very own male enhancement journey!

CHAPTER 1: WHY IS PENIS SIZE SO IMPORTANT?

In different cultures throughout history, men have always placed a lot of importance on the size of the penis. In some cultures, large penises symbolized several positive attributes such as strength, power, courage, masculinity, etc. We can see phallic images pretty much everywhere in the world.

The adoration of phallic imagery dates back to millennia, and even nowadays, people still celebrate and worship the male organ. For instance, the Kanamara Matsuri festival in Kawasaki, Japan, also known as the "Festival of the Steel phallus" is celebrated on the first Sunday of April to encourage fertility among couples.

Never before in history have men been so preoccupied with the size of their genitals. A lot of men are willing to go to extreme lengths to gain some size below the belt. Believing that your size is not adequate can cause severe damage to one's self-esteem. It can affect his confidence not only in the bedroom but even in his social life as well.

Some men are so self-conscious and worried that their size is not adequate, that they start avoiding places like public urinals or shared bathrooms. They fear to expose their penis and getting ridiculed by others. Some men even avoid having sex if they feel that their penis size is less than ideal.

What shapes our size expectations?

Most men form their opinions about penis size during their childhood years. As boys, first may see and compare their penis to that of their brother or father and think that they have a small penis.

This belief can be hard to change even after puberty when the penis increases in size.

A lot of fears related to penis size may be caused by the ridicule of others during the early years too. For instance, some boys that are late bloomers and thus develop until a later age might be a target of ridicule of other boys with bigger penises. The anxiety and fear that results from this teasing will probably haunt them for years, if not decades.

Some boys at a young age might have read what the average penis size should be, and then measure their penis, just to become disappointed. They haven't realized that the penis size they are comparing to is adult-sized penises and that they still haven't developed fully. Men that measure their penis while flaccid will create additional anxiety because they aren't aware that they should have measured while fully erect.

Men and boys are also more exposed to pornography nowadays than before. Male pornstars typically tend to be well-endowed, as it is a desirable attribute for making adult movies that sell better. Outside of professional pornography, most men that upload homemade adult videos tend to be those that have larger than average penises. It is not common for a man with average or small penis size to upload a video that exposes their penis, as they typically want to avoid being the target of negative comments.

Men that look at porn, both professional and homemade, might think that the average male has a penis that is much bigger than what he currently has, further damaging their perception of what reality is.

Other factors affect our perspective of what the penis size should be. Because men tend to look at their penises from above, it usually looks slightly smaller than it is.

To have a clear idea of what your real size is, you would need to look at your penis through the reflection of a full-length mirror.

What is the real average penis size?

Most penis measurements published as part of studies have been done on adults and rarely on teenagers. The reasoning is that everyone grows at a different rate. What's the point in measuring the penis size of developing teenagers? There will be lots of variabilities. It is common for boy's testicles to grow between the ages of 11 to 18. Usually, the testes tend to develop first, before the penis. The penis doesn't reach its full length until a man reaches 21 years of age.

For adult men, the average non-erect penis size tends to be around 3.6 inches (9.16cm) and 5.16 inches (13.12 cm) when erect.

There is more variance with thickness. Standard flaccid width tends to vary from 3.5 to 3.9 inches (9 to 10 cm), while erect girth tends to be around 4.7 inches (12cm).

It is critical to be aware that a man's flaccid penis size is a very poor indicator of his erect size. You have probably heard of the terms "grower" and "shower." A "shower" is a man that has an excellent flaccid penis size, but it doesn't grow too much when fully erect. On the other hand, a "grower" is a man that has an unimpressive flaccid penis size, but it tends to grow and become much more prominent when erect.

To measure the penis, use a ruler or measuring tape. If you're using a ruler, make sure that it's a solid one, and press it into your groin and measure your penis from the base to the tip of the glans. The easiest way to measure width is by using a measuring tape and wrapping it around the fullest part of the penis.

Regardless of this fact, a lot of men tend to feel very unhappy with the size of their penis. There have been studies made where researchers ask up to fifty thousand men if they're satisfied with their current size. 45% of them answered that they would be happier if they had a bigger penis. Interestingly enough, some studies have shown that concerns and anxiety about penis size tend to be higher in men with average-sized penises than among males with smaller dimensions.

Race and penis size

We've known for a while now that different ethnicities have different penis sizes. The stereotype of "most African men have larger penises than average" has been greatly exaggerated, but has some truth to it. The same goes to the stereotype of "Asian men tend to have smaller penises while western men tend to fall somewhere in the middle of the scale."

The subject of race and penis size has been hotly debated and widely researched. One of the most significant studies made on this topic studied 113 different nationalities and measured their average penis lengths.

It seems like Africans as a whole do indeed have a larger penis size than other ethnicities, but the differences can be quite significant among various African countries. For instance, the country with the overall biggest average penis size is the Republic of Congo with 7.1 inches. However, some Hispanic countries such as Ecuador and Colombia beat several of the countries that have primarily an African population.

Western countries such as the United States, Australia, Germany, and the United Kingdom seem to be right in the middle of the list, with an average penis length hovering around 5 inches.

The countries at the bottom of the list, those with the smallest average penis size are India, Thailand, and North and South Korea with average penis lengths of 4 inches or less.

The influence of other factors

Other factors, such as age, weight, and height, have been researched to see if they have any connection to penis size.

There seems not to be a correlation among age and penile dimensions among adults. After a male reaches age 21, the penis remains relatively the same, even after a few decades later. In some cases, some men might see a slight decrease in penis width after reaching 50 years of age. The reduction might be more related to other health conditions, though, such as erectile dysfunction. Men that are over age 50 tend to experience usually have worse blood flow than younger men.

This might explain the small reduction in penis size, as worse blood flow equals worse erection quality.

The connection between weight and penis size might not be complicated to explain. When a man is overweight or obese, the fat at the base of the penis will hide part of the shaft. It is not uncommon for men that have lost a lot of weight to gain half an inch or a full extra inch. Being overweight or obese can also cause diminished blood flow and thus fewer firm erections, making the penis appear smaller than it can be.

For a long time, people have thought that it is possible to predict penis size by looking at a man's hand, finger length or foot size. Some believe that large fingers or a large shoe size equal a large penis. However, most of these connections have been proven to be wrong. Height is the only predictable factor that has some connection with penis size. Taller men have been found to have bigger penises.

However, the influence of height isn't that much to be relevant. Most tall men have averagely sized penises.

When is a penis considered truly small?

The answer might depend on who you are asking. For instance, if you ask physicians, a penis is considered small when it's a candidate for a size augmentation procedure, which is around 3 inches erect. Men that are above 3 inches usually aren't allowed to get surgery, because it can be a risky and controversial procedure.

However, there is a term called "micropenis," that applies only to around .6% of males that have tiny penises. This condition can be tough on most males that have it. It is usually caused by factors that interfere with penis growth while a baby is inside his mother's womb. The penis first starts growing when a fetus is around eight weeks old.

By the twelfth week, the fetus's penis has developed, and it starts to grow. Certain male sex hormones are responsible for continuing the growth of the penis during the second trimester and onward. When certain factors interfere with male hormone production, this can severely stunt penis growth.

Hormone therapy is beneficial for treating micropenis in babies. For instance, testosterone therapy can work wonders to stimulate penis growth during childhood and after puberty. Adults with micropenis have few options, as hormone therapy does very little at that point. Fortunately, for most men, a micropenis is a very rare condition. Most men that believe they have a small penis, probably have average or just slightly below averagely sized penises.

There is even something called "small-penis syndrome": being convinced of having a smaller penis than it is or feeling that you're not man enough because of your penis size.

Besides penis surgery and the methods that we will see and discuss in this book, there is also a lot of promise with regenerative medicine. While it is still in its infancy, there have been experiments made with regenerative medicine, where new tissue is grown from a patient's scrotal skin. This skin is then grafted to the penis to increase its size.

What do women think of penis size?

By far, males seem to be much more worried about penis size than females do. This is interesting because the ultimate fear of those unsure of their size is not able to please their partner well, and that only a giant penis will do the job.

The research done on this topic has concluded that around 85% of women are satisfied with their partner's size.

As mentioned previously, at least 45% of men either believe that they have a small penis that is insufficient to please their partner or would like to have a larger penis.

This doesn't mean that women don't care about size, but how much they care has been greatly exaggerated by men and the media. For a clear minority of women, though, size matters more than usual.

One particular experiment on the subject took several women and showed them over 30 different penis dimensions with the use of 3d printing. The sizes varied a lot, from 4 inches to almost 9 inches in length.

Women seemed to prefer penis size based on the type of relationship they had in mind. For long term partners, women went for just over 6 inches in length and a width of around 4.8 inches. For short term relationships or one night stands, they preferred the slightly larger penises.

However, the difference wasn't night and day: 6.4 inches and a thickness of 5 inches.

Interestingly enough, women seem to care more about penis width than size, according to some studies. The width appears to be more correlated with sexual satisfaction than length.

The penis and evolution

While it seems that for women, a large penis isn't at the top of the list when searching for a long term or short term partner (more important priorities for them are factors such as height, shoulder to waist ratio, etc), it does matter slightly.

Early humans didn't wear clothes as we now do, and penises were exposed, and the size was evident to females.

We know that men nowadays have larger penises than early men, so undoubtedly there has been some natural selection going on. This not exclusively means that women have historically chosen men with larger penis size, though.

Some researchers mention that the penis has evolved to its current spear-like shape to better scoop rival male semen from a woman's reproductive tract. Deeper trusting better displaces rival semen than shallow thrusting, which might partially explain why men nowadays have bigger genitals than their ancestors.

The bottom line

After reading this chapter, you might have felt a sense of relief to hear about how wrong men tend to be about their size and its importance for pleasing a partner. You also might be wondering if there is anything you can do about the current size of your penis.

After all, there is nothing wrong with wanting to have a larger penis. If you feel like your overall sense of happiness would improve if you had a larger penis, then, by all means, you should go for this goal.

Mainstream belief is that you are pretty much stuck with the size you've got. Men that have been blessed with a large penis are part of a lucky group that the vast majority of men will never access. Surprisingly, there's a great deal that you can do to alter your current penis measurements. These options remain mostly unknown to most people.

Knowing exactly how to increase the size of your penis successfully can be life-altering information. Very few men are aware of this knowledge, and so it will be an eye-opening experience for most.

By the end of this book, you will know exactly what to do to increase the length and girth of your penis if you wish to do so, as you will know the right techniques that have been proven to give good results time and again. You will also know how to cure or relieve a lot of the most common male sexual problems so that you won't have to worry and stress out before or during sex ever again.

CHAPTER 2: DISPELLING MYTHS AND FALSE BELIEF ABOUT PENIS ENLARGEMENT

One look at the male enhancement industry is enough to confuse anyone: penis pills, penis pumps, surgery, clamps. With so many options available, along with the number of frauds and scams, it can be extremely arriving at the truth.

A lot of the products related to male enhancement can be costly. Also, the penis is a complex organ with lots of sensitive tissue, that one shouldn't be experimenting with it.

In this chapter, we will be taking an in-depth look at some of the most popular options available in the male enhancement industry. Many of these products promise to add size to the penis or boost your sex life. Doing this will help clear a lot of doubts and will also let you understand better how the male enhancement industry works. In the end, you will know what to stay away from and what will genuinely help you grow a few inches.

Penis pills

Probably the most infamous product in the male enhancement industry is penis pills. The average male with internet access has perhaps seen countless penis pill ads for most of his life. A quick visit to an adult site will probably expose you to advertisements of pills that promise to add incredible amounts of length and thickness to your penis in the blink of an eye. Ads of pills that promise to add a couple of inches in less than two weeks aren't uncommon.

Most men do approach these products with a good deal of skepticism. After all, they all sound too good to be true. Some of the most desperate ones end up purchasing these products.

So what's the deal with penis pills? Do they work a little, or not at all? Are they dangerous? In reality, there is no evidence that penis pills can give you long-lasting growth. In some of the cases, the penis pills can even pose a threat to your health.

It is common for penis pills to include certain "sneaky" ingredients such as maca or horny goat weed. These aren't typically dangerous, but they are substances that help improve erection quality and sexual desire while taking them. They can be a pretty good way to enhance one's sex life if looking for a boost in bedroom performance. However, they do very little to give actual long-lasting increments to penis size.

So why do penis pills sometimes offer a 30-day money-back guarantee or similar refund policy? The effects caused by the male enhancement pills can give the illusion of giving you more size thanks to the short term improvements in erection quality, firmness, and strength. Those that take these pills and notice these improvements usually equate these changes to real long term penis growth.

There is no reason to use penis pills if you're mainly interested in male enhancement. If you are interested in boosting your sex life, then some of the pills might do the trick. In any case, there are much better and safer options available. If you decide to use any of these products, it's best to consult with your physician and check if there are no potential side effects from the included ingredients.

Surgical procedures

Out of all the male enhancement options, surgical procedures are probably the ones that people believe that can have the most legit results. There is quite a bit of truth in this. A well-prepared surgeon with demonstrated cases of success can potentially change the life of a lot of men.

But just as with most medical surgeries, there is always the possibility of complications or unwanted side effects. There is still a risk involved. There have been cases of temporal or permanent erectile dysfunction happening after a male enhancement surgical procedure. Several other complications may occur if the patient doesn't take proper care of himself after the surgery. Of course, complications aren't the norm, but anyone interested in such procedures should be well aware that they are a definite possibility.

As a whole, male enhancement surgery is well beyond the scope of this book and is a broad medical topic in itself. But the bottom line is that you should only use it as a last resource. Some men might be tempted to try surgery because it can be an instant solution to their problem. In most cases, however, undergoing surgery is only recommended in specific situations (such as for those that have the micropenis condition) or after trying several other methods first.

Penis extenders

In the male enhancement industry, there are lots of devices available that promise to add several inches to your penis. Some of them have the added benefit of being able to be worn while you are performing other activities, such as working or doing chores at home.

One of the most popular devices is penis extenders.

These are devices that you set and forget and promise to add length after some time. Many of these devices recommend users to expect results after six months or a year.

The idea of using a device to increase penis size is not a new concept. Several cultures around the world have experimented with using tools that increase the size of certain parts of their bodies, such as earlobes or lips.

The way these devices work is by applying very little continuous resistance to the tissue over some time. For instance, in some cultures where a long neck is desirable, people add rings to the neck until they reach the desired length. This process usually takes years.

You might also have seen people with enlarged earlobes. At first, they tend to use earrings that expand their earlobe and increase the size of the earrings as the earlobe tissue grows more and more.

There are some cultures have experimented with increasing the size of their penises similarly. Some of these cultures attach heavy objects such as rocks to their penises to apply constant pressure.

Extender devices in the male enhancement industry work similarly to the above. They apply resistance on the penis over a set period. The force applied to the tissue increase the size of the penis through adaptation. You need to wear these devices for several hours per day, the typical range being between 30 mins to 8 hours, depending on your toleration levels. Beginners might only be able to wear these devices for 30 mins, whereas more advanced users can wear them for several hours with little to no discomfort. Typically, you can see results after at least six months of continuous use.

Penis extenders can be bulky devices, and although there are some convenient ones available, some can be a bit uncomfortable to use. It's almost impossible to use an extender under tight pieces of clothing.

Most people with a typical day job will find that it is tough to use them discreetly and comfortably. These devices tend to give good results, but only to those that can wear them consistently, for several hours per day, over at least six months or more. They can also be very expensive. There are some budget options available, but they can sometimes be more uncomfortable or not as safe as the more expensive ones. Suitable devices with solid research and user experience backing them up are hard to find for cheap.

If you can wear one of these devices for prolonged periods and are interested in acquiring one, then never go for a little known brand. With male enhancement, it's always best to err on the side of caution, as it is crucial to avoid any short or long term damage.

Extenders can be a great option and are well worthy of consideration if you're interested in adding a few inches to your penis without doing much work.

Another critical thing to keep in mind is that extenders will mostly give you length gains. While some men do experience girth gains from them, it is not the norm.

Other options will be probably better for most, as the drawbacks of cost, time, and discomfort might be too much for many.

Penis pumps

The two main types of penis pumps are air-based and water-based pumps.

Air-based pumps have been used to treat erectile dysfunction for a while now. They are even well known by mainstream consumers that haven't dived deep into the world of male enhancement. The use of air-based pumps can also prolong ejaculation and improve sexual desire.

Although not commonly used mainly for increasing size, some men have reported gains after extended use of such products.

Air pumps do have some drawbacks though. The main disadvantage is that after reaching a specific vacuum level with the device, there can be edema accumulation in the penis after some use. Edema can quickly build up under the skin when using air-based pumps and cause discoloration or feelings of discomfort and soreness in the genital area. There can be some workarounds to avoid edema build-up, but they are not always practical or straightforward.

Some advantages of air-based pumps are that they can be relatively inexpensive when compared to other options. Because of this, they can be a decent option for people with a limited budget that would like to use a device that will likely boost their sexual performance.

However, many consider air-based pumps to be obsolete, considering that there are other "better" devices available, such as water-based pumps, which we'll get to next.

Water-based pumps

In the world of male enhancement, water-based pumps have been increasing in sales and popularity every year, because they provide users with several short and long term benefits. A lot of people believe that they are superior in every way to air-based pumps, as they arguably offer more advantages and fewer disadvantages in most cases.

As the name implies, water-based pumps create a vacuum by using warm water instead of air. You can use them while taking a shower or a bath.

The water vacuum created by these devices can be quite intense, and it can force a lot of blood flow inside the corpus cavernosum of the penis. It can force much more blood inside the penis than what the average male can achieve via a healthy erection through sexual arousal.

Some proponents of water-based pumps mention that the lymphatic system gets some benefits too. Water-based pumps help promote the oxidation of blood cells, which help flush out toxins and improve penis health. The problem of edema build-up is still present with water-based pumps, but significantly less so when compared to air-based pumps.

Water-based pumps also improve overall male sexual health: because of the increased blood flow, erection quality, sexual desire, and stamina tend to develop as well. The main reason why men buy water-based pumps is that they provide both short and long term benefits.

After using a water-based pump for a single session, users will notice an immediate temporal gain in penis size and erection quality. A lot of men like to use these devices right before having sex. An immediate increase in penis size is one of the most attractive features of water-based pumps, as most devices take months or even years to show results.

With long term use, water-based pumps can also increase penis size; however, the gains will mostly be in thickness and not in length.

The final word on water-based pumps is that they do work. They are one of the few devices in the market that can give both short term and long term benefits. They can also help people that are suffering from erectile dysfunction by increasing blood flow inside the penis. The main drawbacks are that these devices tend to be a bit expensive, especially models with a good reputation. They are also very bulky devices, and you can only wear them while showering or bathing.

Penis Hanging devices

Penis hanging is one of the most ancient forms of male enhancement known. It involves using a tool that creates tension by hanging a weight on the penis that will develop micro-tears. These micro-tears, when repaired, will promote cell growth, causing penis growth over time.

Penis hanging is mostly used to increase length, but some users have reported girth improvements as well.

Penis hanging works similarly to penis extender devices, but there is a crucial difference: hanging tools place lots of tension in a small amount of time. Penis extenders put very little resistance, and you have to wear them for a very long time to see results. They work by applying minimal resistance over long periods, while penis hanging works the opposite way: by using a lot of tension over short sessions. Applying too much resistance over long periods would only cause damage to the penis tissue.

A lot of proponents of penis hanging claim that when performed correctly, it can be a safe method of male enhancement. Others believe that penis hanging should be avoided because it is easy to go overboard or do things wrong and damage the penis. The same people tend to think that there are better and safer options out there.

A great thing about this method is that you can have complete control of the amount of tension that you will use during a session. Similar to exercising in the gym, where you pick up the weight that you know will work out your muscles the best, hanging gives you a lot of control over the amount of tension used. Most forms of male enhancement do not give you this option and involve a lot of guesswork and intuition.

Advanced users of male enhancement should be the only ones performing penis hanging. At least 6 to 8 months of conditioning with other methods is highly recommended. It does require users to have a better understanding of their body and limits before starting.

Penis Clamping

Penis clamping is one of those methods that most users agree should o advanced users only. It is mainly used for increasing the thickness of the penis. So why is it considered risky and isn't recommended for beginners?

The way clamping works is by using a device to build up a lot of pressure inside the penis and restrict blood flow while also allowing inflow but in minimal amounts. After doing this for a few sessions, the pressure forced inside the penis will force the tissue into growing via adaptation.

There can be some complications and injuries by not practicing this method safely: vein thrombosis and lymph vessels. When the penis tissue is not used to the enormous amounts of pressure that clamping caused, you can easily injure yourself and cause some painful damage.

With enough time, clamping works. It forces the penis into a size beyond its standard capabilities. However, it is an option that should be exclusively reserved for very advanced users, as there are much more practical and safer methods available.

Exercises

It may be a difficult concept to wrap your head around that the penis can be exercised. As you have read, many of the above methods work. They do this by placing pressure or by forcing blood flow inside the penis, both of which may trigger growth. Well, there are several ways to do the same thing by just using your hands and not needing to spend anything.

A lot of manual penis exercises are not only very convenient, but they are also safe, healthy, and the best part: they are completely free. The benefits are enormous, and the drawbacks are very few.

Besides size gains, manual exercises can give you an overall improvement in male sexual health: erection quality, stamina, and libido all tend to improve after the safe practice of vigorous enhancement exercises.

There are lots of different manual exercises that can be used for pretty much every goal. Whether you're looking for length gains, girth gains, better erections, or even improved resting size gain. They can be performed almost anywhere as long as you can be in a private place. They also don't require large amounts of time to see real gains. Some men have even reported seeing visible results after a few weeks of performing them!

The male enhancement section of this guide focuses mainly on the best and most effective exercises and routines that you can use to achieve your desired size goals. Throughout the next chapter, we will take an in-depth look at the best exercises that have the highest rate of success among users.

We will also take a look at different exercise routines that you can use to continue progressing. Male enhancement is very similar to exercising your muscles. After a while, there will be some degree of adaptation; to keep improving, you must change things up in an efficient manner.

Because male enhancement exercises are efficient and free, you can start performing them today if you wish to do so. There is probably no better way to begin your enhancement journey! You might even choose to use some of the other options mentioned in this chapter afterward. But being acquainted with the basic exercises may be all you need to achieve your desired size.

There are many, many more male enhancement options available, and covering them all would be no easy task. However, we've already looked at the options that are the most popular and widely used of them all.

CHAPTER 3: THE BEST MALE ENHANCEMENT EXERCISES

One look at the male enhancement industry is enough to confuse anyone: penis pills, penis pumps, surgery, clamps. With so many options available, along with the number of frauds and scams, it can be extremely arriving at the truth.

A lot of the products related to male enhancement can be costly. Also, the penis is a complex organ with lots of sensitive tissue, that one shouldn't be experimenting with it.

In this chapter, we will be taking an in-depth look at some of the most popular options available in the male enhancement industry. Many of these products promise to add size to the penis or boost your sex life. Doing this will help clear a lot of doubts and will also let you understand better how the male enhancement industry works. In the end, you will know what to stay away from and what will genuinely help you grow a few inches.

Penis pills

Probably the most infamous product in the male enhancement industry is penis pills. The average male with internet access has perhaps seen countless penis pill ads for most of his life. A quick visit to an adult site will probably expose you to advertisements of pills that promise to add incredible amounts of length and thickness to your penis in the blink of an eye. Ads of pills that promise to add a couple of inches in less than two weeks aren't uncommon.

Most men do approach these products with a good deal of skepticism. After all, they all sound too good to be true. Some of the most desperate ones end up purchasing these products.

So what's the deal with penis pills? Do they work a little, or not at all? Are they dangerous? In reality, there is no evidence that penis pills can give you long-lasting growth. In some of the cases, the penis pills can even pose a threat to your health.

It is common for penis pills to include certain "sneaky" ingredients such as maca or horny goat weed. These aren't typically dangerous, but they are substances that help improve erection quality and sexual desire while taking them. They can be a pretty good way to enhance one's sex life if looking for a boost in bedroom performance. However, they do very little to give actual long-lasting increments to penis size.

So why do penis pills sometimes offer a 30-day money-back guarantee or similar refund policy? The effects caused by the male enhancement pills can give the illusion of giving you more size thanks to the short term improvements in erection quality, firmness, and strength. Those that take these pills and notice these improvements usually equate these changes to real long term penis growth.

There is no reason to use penis pills if you're mainly interested in male enhancement. If you are interested in boosting your sex life, then some of the pills might do the trick. In any case, there are much better and safer options available. If you decide to use any of these products, it's best to consult with your physician and check if there are no potential side effects from the included ingredients.

Surgical procedures

Out of all the male enhancement options, surgical procedures are probably the ones that people believe that can have the most legit results. There is quite a bit of truth in this. A well-prepared surgeon with demonstrated cases of success can potentially change the life of a lot of men.

But just as with most medical surgeries, there is always the possibility of complications or unwanted side effects. There is still a risk involved. There have been cases of temporal or permanent erectile dysfunction happening after a male enhancement surgical procedure. Several other complications may occur if the patient doesn't take proper care of himself after the surgery. Of course, complications aren't the norm, but anyone interested in such procedures should be well aware that they are a definite possibility.

As a whole, male enhancement surgery is well beyond the scope of this book and is a broad medical topic in itself. But the bottom line is that you should only use it as a last resource. Some men might be tempted to try surgery because it can be an instant solution to their problem. In most cases, however, undergoing surgery is only recommended in specific situations (such as for those that have the micropenis condition) or after trying several other methods first.

Penis extenders

In the male enhancement industry, there are lots of devices available that promise to add several inches to your penis. Some of them have the added benefit of being able to be worn while you are performing other activities, such as working or doing chores at home.

One of the most popular devices is penis extenders.

These are devices that you set and forget and promise to add length after some time. Many of these devices recommend users to expect results after six months or a year.

The idea of using a device to increase penis size is not a new concept. Several cultures around the world have experimented with using tools that increase the size of certain parts of their bodies, such as earlobes or lips.

The way these devices work is by applying very little continuous resistance to the tissue over some time. For instance, in some cultures where a long neck is desirable, people add rings to the neck until they reach the desired length. This process usually takes years.

You might also have seen people with enlarged earlobes. At first, they tend to use earrings that expand their earlobe and increase the size of the earrings as the earlobe tissue grows more and more.

There are some cultures have experimented with increasing the size of their penises similarly. Some of these cultures attach heavy objects such as rocks to their penises to apply constant pressure.

Extender devices in the male enhancement industry work similarly to the above. They apply resistance on the penis over a set period. The force applied to the tissue increase the size of the penis through adaptation. You need to wear these devices for several hours per day, the typical range being between 30 mins to 8 hours, depending on your toleration levels. Beginners might only be able to wear these devices for 30 mins, whereas more advanced users can wear them for several hours with little to no discomfort. Typically, you can see results after at least six months of continuous use.

Penis extenders can be bulky devices, and although there are some convenient ones available, some can be a bit uncomfortable to use. It's almost impossible to use an extender under tight pieces of clothing.

Most people with a typical day job will find that it is tough to use them discreetly and comfortably. These devices tend to give good results, but only to those that can wear them consistently, for several hours per day, over at least six months or more. They can also be very expensive. There are some budget options available, but they can sometimes be more uncomfortable or not as safe as the more expensive ones. Suitable devices with solid research and user experience backing them up are hard to find for cheap.

If you can wear one of these devices for prolonged periods and are interested in acquiring one, then never go for a little known brand. With male enhancement, it's always best to err on the side of caution, as it is crucial to avoid any short or long term damage.

Extenders can be a great option and are well worthy of consideration if you're interested in adding a few inches to your penis without doing much work.

Another critical thing to keep in mind is that extenders will mostly give you length gains. While some men do experience girth gains from them, it is not the norm.

Other options will be probably better for most, as the drawbacks of cost, time, and discomfort might be too much for many.

Penis pumps

The two main types of penis pumps are air-based and water-based pumps.

Air-based pumps have been used to treat erectile dysfunction for a while now. They are even well known by mainstream consumers that haven't dived deep into the world of male enhancement. The use of air-based pumps can also prolong ejaculation and improve sexual desire.

Although not commonly used mainly for increasing size, some men have reported gains after extended use of such products.

Air pumps do have some drawbacks though. The main disadvantage is that after reaching a specific vacuum level with the device, there can be edema accumulation in the penis after some use. Edema can quickly build up under the skin when using air-based pumps and cause discoloration or feelings of discomfort and soreness in the genital area. There can be some workarounds to avoid edema build-up, but they are not always practical or straightforward.

Some advantages of air-based pumps are that they can be relatively inexpensive when compared to other options. Because of this, they can be a decent option for people with a limited budget that would like to use a device that will likely boost their sexual performance.

However, many consider air-based pumps to be obsolete, considering that there are other "better" devices available, such as water-based pumps, which we'll get to next.

Water-based pumps

In the world of male enhancement, water-based pumps have been increasing in sales and popularity every year, because they provide users with several short and long term benefits. A lot of people believe that they are superior in every way to air-based pumps, as they arguably offer more advantages and fewer disadvantages in most cases.

As the name implies, water-based pumps create a vacuum by using warm water instead of air. You can use them while taking a shower or a bath.

The water vacuum created by these devices can be quite intense, and it can force a lot of blood flow inside the corpus cavernosum of the penis. It can force much more blood inside the penis than what the average male can achieve via a healthy erection through sexual arousal.

Some proponents of water-based pumps mention that the lymphatic system gets some benefits too. Water-based pumps help promote the oxidation of blood cells, which help flush out toxins and improve penis health. The problem of edema build-up is still present with water-based pumps, but significantly less so when compared to air-based pumps.

Water-based pumps also improve overall male sexual health: because of the increased blood flow, erection quality, sexual desire, and stamina tend to develop as well. The main reason why men buy water-based pumps is that they provide both short and long term benefits.

After using a water-based pump for a single session, users will notice an immediate temporal gain in penis size and erection quality. A lot of men like to use these devices right before having sex. An immediate increase in penis size is one of the most attractive features of water-based pumps, as most devices take months or even years to show results.

With long term use, water-based pumps can also increase penis size; however, the gains will mostly be in thickness and not in length.

The final word on water-based pumps is that they do work. They are one of the few devices in the market that can give both short term and long term benefits. They can also help people that are suffering from erectile dysfunction by increasing blood flow inside the penis. The main drawbacks are that these devices tend to be a bit expensive, especially models with a good reputation. They are also very bulky devices, and you can only wear them while showering or bathing.

Penis Hanging devices

Penis hanging is one of the most ancient forms of male enhancement known. It involves using a tool that creates tension by hanging a weight on the penis that will develop micro-tears. These micro-tears, when repaired, will promote cell growth, causing penis growth over time.

Penis hanging is mostly used to increase length, but some users have reported girth improvements as well.

Penis hanging works similarly to penis extender devices, but there is a crucial difference: hanging tools place lots of tension in a small amount of time. Penis extenders put very little resistance, and you have to wear them for a very long time to see results. They work by applying minimal resistance over long periods, while penis hanging works the opposite way: by using a lot of tension over short sessions. Applying too much resistance over long periods would only cause damage to the penis tissue.

A lot of proponents of penis hanging claim that when performed correctly, it can be a safe method of male enhancement. Others believe that penis hanging should be avoided because it is easy to go overboard or do things wrong and damage the penis. The same people tend to think that there are better and safer options out there.

A great thing about this method is that you can have complete control of the amount of tension that you will use during a session. Similar to exercising in the gym, where you pick up the weight that you know will work out your muscles the best, hanging gives you a lot of control over the amount of tension used. Most forms of male enhancement do not give you this option and involve a lot of guesswork and intuition.

Advanced users of male enhancement should be the only ones performing penis hanging. At least 6 to 8 months of conditioning with other methods is highly recommended. It does require users to have a better understanding of their body and limits before starting.

Penis Clamping

Penis clamping is one of those methods that most users agree should o advanced users only. It is mainly used for increasing the thickness of the penis. So why is it considered risky and isn't recommended for beginners?

The way clamping works is by using a device to build up a lot of pressure inside the penis and restrict blood flow while also allowing inflow but in minimal amounts. After doing this for a few sessions, the pressure forced inside the penis will force the tissue into growing via adaptation.

There can be some complications and injuries by not practicing this method safely: vein thrombosis and lymph vessels. When the penis tissue is not used to the enormous amounts of pressure that clamping caused, you can easily injure yourself and cause some painful damage.

With enough time, clamping works. It forces the penis into a size beyond its standard capabilities. However, it is an option that should be exclusively reserved for very advanced users, as there are much more practical and safer methods available.

Exercises

It may be a difficult concept to wrap your head around that the penis can be exercised. As you have read, many of the above methods work. They do this by placing pressure or by forcing blood flow inside the penis, both of which may trigger growth. Well, there are several ways to do the same thing by just using your hands and not needing to spend anything.

A lot of manual penis exercises are not only very convenient, but they are also safe, healthy, and the best part: they are completely free. The benefits are enormous, and the drawbacks are very few.

Besides size gains, manual exercises can give you an overall improvement in male sexual health: erection quality, stamina, and libido all tend to improve after the safe practice of vigorous enhancement exercises.

There are lots of different manual exercises that can be used for pretty much every goal. Whether you're looking for length gains, girth gains, better erections, or even improved resting size gain. They can be performed almost anywhere as long as you can be in a private place. They also don't require large amounts of time to see real gains. Some men have even reported seeing visible results after a few weeks of performing them!

The male enhancement section of this guide focuses mainly on the best and most effective exercises and routines that you can use to achieve your desired size goals. Throughout the next chapter, we will take an in-depth look at the best exercises that have the highest rate of success among users.

We will also take a look at different exercise routines that you can use to continue progressing. Male enhancement is very similar to exercising your muscles. After a while, there will be some degree of adaptation; to keep improving, you must change things up in an efficient manner.

Because male enhancement exercises are efficient and free, you can start performing them today if you wish to do so. There is probably no better way to begin your enhancement journey! You might even choose to use some of the other options mentioned in this chapter afterward. But being acquainted with the basic exercises may be all you need to achieve your desired size.

There are many, many more male enhancement options available, and covering them all would be no easy task. However, we've already looked at the options that are the most popular and widely used of them all.

CHAPTER 4: THE BEST PROGRAM FOR BEGINNERS

If you are interested in making size gains, then you must realize that the first few months are the most crucial ones that will determine your success. For most men, the correct selection of male enhancement exercises will give them excellent results during the first three to four months. Just as with training with weights in the gym, complete newbies tend to quickly get what some call "beginner gains" or "newbie gains." These are gains that will come very fast and will also condition your genitals for more advanced exercises in the future.

If you have never performed any male enhancement program before, we greatly suggest that you don't skip the beginner program. The exercises and frequency of the beginner program have been carefully selected to promote growth in an unconditioned penis while avoiding any side effects or setbacks that may occur from overtraining or using motions that are best suited for advanced users.

So how long should you stick with the beginner program? As a minimum, we recommend sticking with it for at least three months. Even better if you can stick with it for 3 or 4 months. Also, feel free to go back to it any time you want to get a boost in penile health. Most male enhancement exercises that you'll use for size gains can be used to promote better erections, stamina, ejaculation control, etc.

A lot of men are only interested in adding a bit of size to their penis.

If so, then doing the beginner's program is likely more than enough for them and probably all they would ever need. If you feel like you would like to continue gaining more size after sticking with the beginner's program for at least 3-4 months, then it's time to move on to the more advanced routines included in this book.

Frequency

So how often should the beginner's routine be performed? It is typically recommended to perform this routine every day for five days in a row and then to rest for two days. Some men can tolerate more and might do well with six days of exercising and resting for only one. Although this program doesn't take much time at all, those that have hectic lives can get away with great gains even if they only perform the routine for two days in a row and then rest for one.

Warming-up

The warm-up phase is often not included in some male enhancement programs, but this can be a very costly mistake in a lot of cases. A lot of men aren't used to the kind of stress that male enhancement exercises place on their penis tissue, and because of this, they might run into a lot of setbacks just because they forgot to include a warm-up. A proper warm-up does a lot to condition and prepares the tissues for more intense exercises. 5-10 minutes of warm-up will be more than enough for most.

To warm-up, we recommend getting a piece of cloth and some mildly hot water (make sure it's only moderately hot with your hands, you do not want to burn yourself down there!). Start by taking the cloth and fully moistening it with the hot water. Then take the cloth and apply it to your whole genital and pubic region. The hot water should reach everything, especially the areas that will be exercised the most: the penis base, entire shaft, gland, and even the testicles.

The pubic region should also be thoroughly moistened. The key here is to prepare all the tissues and ligaments for the exercises that will come later.

After applying the hot towel for a while, the moistened areas will start to feel a bit hot from inside. This feeling is the cue that lets you know that you are now prepared to move on and start with the exercises.

The first real exercise you will perform will be helicopter shakes. As you now know, this exercise is excellent to get the tissue and ligaments loose and ready for more intense things. Performing the following two sets of helicopter shakes should take you no longer than three to five minutes.

Exercise set #1. Helicopter shakes.

Do at least 70 repetitions clockwise.

Do at least 70 repetitions counter-clockwise.

Moving on, the next exercise that you should perform is the basic penis stretch. Manual stretches are an excellent option to perform after proper warm-up and prep because they don't stress the penis as much as other exercises such as jelqing do. As you can see, we are slowly ramping up the intensity with the exercise selection.

You can perform manual stretches at lots of different angles, and it is crucial to cover a lot of them because this will force the tissue and ligaments to grow at a much quicker rate than if you only focused in the same position.

Tip: We recommend using a timer instead of trying to guess for how long you've been pulling the penis.

Exercise set #2. Basic penis stretches. First-round.

Remember that you should never feel any pain doing any of these exercises. Refer to the exercises chapters if you need a reminder on how to perform them correctly.

As a reference, imagine that you are staring at a typical clock.

Grab your penis and pull it down (6 o´clock position) for 23 seconds

Grab your penis and pull it up (noon position) for 23 seconds

Grab your penis and pull it to the right (3 o´clock position) for 23 seconds

Grab your penis and pull it to the left (9 o´clock position) for 23 seconds

After finishing the above four motions, grab and stretch the penis from the upwards noon position, and proceed to make a complete circle with your penis while keeping the pulling tension on it at all times. Perform the circle very slowly. Doing a full circle typically takes anywhere from 40 to 60 seconds.

Exercise set #3. Basic penis stretches. Second-round.

Grab your penis and pull it up and to the right (1 o´clock position) for 23 seconds

Grab your penis and pull it up to the right (2 o´clock position) for 23 seconds

Grab your penis and pull it up to the left (11 o´clock position) for 23 seconds

Grab your penis and pull it up to the left (10 o´clock position) for 23 seconds

Grab your penis and pull it down to the right (4 o´clock position) for 23 seconds

Grab your penis and pull it down to the right (5 o´clock position) for 23 seconds

Grab your penis and pull it down to the left (8 o´clock position) for 23 seconds

Grab your penis and pull it down to the left (7 o´clock position) for 23 seconds´

After finishing the above eight motions, grab and stretch the penis from the upwards noon position, and proceed to make a complete circle with your penis while keeping the pulling tension on it at all times. Perform the circle very slowly. This motion should also take anywhere from 40 to 60 seconds.

Jelqing.

After the two sets of manual stretches that you've completed, it is then time to move on to exercises that are more demanding and intense on the penis. The next exercise in the beginner's workout probably the most important out of all of them for overall growth, the jelq.

As mentioned previously, it is highly recommended to use lubricant when performing jelqs and to never go beyond a level 3 erection.

Do keep in mind that it is very easy to get an erection beyond level 3 as you are performing this exercise, as for some it may feel similar to the motions they use when masturbating. If you ever feel like your erection is going beyond level 3, it is best to stop and wait for the blood flow to decrease slightly. Doing this exercise, especially as a newbie with an erection level beyond three, can cause more harm than good. As you get more and more used to the jelqing motion, you should stop having this issue, and you will be able to maintain more or less the same erection level throughout the entire set.

Exercise set #4 Jelqing. Quick reps.

Perform 50 repetitions one after another, by using both hands. Each repetition should only last around one second.

Exercise set #5 Jelqing. Quick reps.

Do 50 repetitions one after another, by using both hands, but this time each repetition should last around 4 seconds.

Once you finish both sets of jelqs, you have two options: you may either warm down or do an extra exercise: v-jelqs. If you are a complete beginner with less than two weeks of experience, we recommend skipping the v-jelqs. After the third or fourth week, incorporating v-jelqs is an excellent option.

Keep in mind that V-jelqs are best done with a lower erection level than standard jelqs. Preferably around a level 2 erection, and never go way beyond that.

Exercise set #6 V-Jelqing.

Perform 20 repetitions one after another, by using both hands, using a noon angle.

Perform 20 repetitions one after another, by using both hands, using a 6 o' clock angle.

Perform 20 repetitions one after another, by using both hands, using a 3 o' clock angle.

Perform 20 repetitions one after another, by using both hands, using a 9 o' clock angle.

The repetitions should last anywhere from 1-3 seconds.

Cooling down

Just as proper warm-up helps prevent injuries and overtraining, cooling down can be crucial to avoid any over exhaustion that may occur in the penis tissue. To cool down properly, grab the cloth and hot water again and do the same as with the warm-up phase, however, this time, you only need to do it for at least 3 minutes.

Important information about overtraining and avoiding setbacks

After you've performed the routine for a few days, it's essential to assess how your body is feeling and check for both positive and negative signs. It is easy to know when you're in the right direction and that you're well on your way to getting some permanent gains. The most important positive sign is when you notice improvements in erection quality. Shortly after a while, you should also start to see an increase in size.

Some new veins might start showing up. If this is the case, then you should continue to do what you've been doing. The path to permanent gains is usually (but not always, as it can vary for each individual) the following: improvement in erection quality > temporary increase in size> permanent increase in size.

On the other hand, if there is a decrease in erection quality, then you are probably going overboard with either the intensity or frequency of the exercises. Whenever you spot this negative sign, it's best to take anywhere from 3-5 days off of doing any male enhancement exercises. Whenever you go back to the exercise routine, you might consider adding more rest days or using less intensity while performing the exercises. If you aren't noticing either positive or negative signs, then you are probably not doing enough to stimulate growth in the penis, so it's a good idea to reduce the rest days or increase the intensity.

For some men, doing male enhancement exercises can be a very smooth ride, and they will rarely encounter any setbacks or notice signs of overtraining. For others, it can be trickier and might reach overtraining or over exhaustion very quickly. In those cases, trial and error is the only solution, as it's essential to find the exact amount of frequency and rest days needed that works for their body. Tolerance to exercise is highly individual and can vary significantly from one person to another.

CHAPTER 5: THE INTERMEDIATE PROGRAM

After doing the beginner program for several months, there will be a point where you will stop seeing any size gains. You will probably still receive some male sexual health benefits such as better erection quality, improved stamina, etc., but the size is likely to remain the same.

Just as with any exercise regime, there will be a point where the body adapts to the levels of stress, and there will be little progress, as the tissue doesn't feel forced to adjust to any new stress. When you reach this point, it is a good idea to move to the intermediate program if you wish to continue making gains. If you are happy with your current size, then it's totally fine if you decide to stop. It's all up to your goals and individual needs.

Warm-up

Being an intermediate doesn't mean that you are now able to skip the warm-up. A proper warm-up will always be essential to avoid setbacks and injuries. A simple 5-10 minute warm-up can make the male enhancement flow a lot more smoothly.

After warming-up, the helicopter shakes from the beginner program can be performed but are entirely optional. If you find that you are overtraining quickly with the intermediate program, then it's a good idea to increase warm-up time, add in the helicopter shakes and maybe decrease the exercise frequency throughout the week. Keep experimenting with these options until you find the sweet spot that helps you continue gaining size.

Exercise set #1. Basic Penis Stretches. First-Round.

Grab your penis and pull it up (noon position) for 34 seconds

Grab your penis and pull it down (6 o´clock position) for 34 seconds

Grab your penis and pull it to the right (3 o´clock position) for 34 seconds

Grab your penis and pull it to the left (9 o´clock position) for 34 seconds

After finishing the above four motions, grab and stretch the penis from the upwards noon position, and proceed to make a complete circle with your penis while keeping the pulling tension on it at all times.

Perform the circle very slowly. Doing a full circle typically takes anywhere from 40 to 60 seconds. How you perform the circle remains unchanged from the beginner's routine.

Exercise set #2. Basic penis stretches. Second-round.

The second set of stretches in the intermediate program will now target the ligaments by using new angles for a profound effect.

Grab and pull the penis under your legs and behind your glutes backward in the center for 34 seconds.

Grab and pull the penis under your legs and behind your glutes backward to the left for 34 seconds.

Grab and pull the penis under your legs and behind your glutes backward to the left for 34 seconds.

After performing these three motions, it's time to do a full circle, but this time by doing it under your legs, behind your glutes. The circle should last anywhere from 40-60 seconds.

Exercise set #4 Jelqing. Quick reps.

It's now time to move on to jelqing. The difference is that you can now perform these with a higher erection level. As always, each body is different and has its unique tolerance level, but it is up to you to experiment. Some men can tolerate performing jelqs with a level 3 erection at this point.

Perform 150 repetitions one after another, by using both hands.

Each repetition should only last around one second.

Exercise set #5 Jelqing. Slow reps.

Perform 100 repetitions one after another, by using both hands. Each repetition should last around four seconds.

Exercise set #6. V-Jelqs.

Perform 35 repetitions one after another, by using both hands, using a noon angle.

Perform 35 repetitions one after another, by using both hands, using a 6 o' clock angle.

Perform 35 repetitions one after another, by using both hands, using a 3 o' clock angle.

Perform 35 repetitions one after another, by using both hands, using a 9 o' clock angle.

End the intermediate program by cooling down the same way as in the beginner's program.

CHAPTER 6: Male enhancement
EXERCISES FOR ADVANCED USERS

As always, the body will continue to grow and adapt to a certain level of stress. After some time, even the intermediate program won't be enough to continue giving you size gains. It is entirely up to you if you'd like to keep gaining some size.

The advanced program has a lot of similarities with the intermediate program, but it has the addition of horse squeezes. Horse squeezes are best left when you have a significant amount of experience with male enhancement as they can cause too much stress in tissue that is not yet ready for them.

Exercise set #1. Basic Penis Stretches. First-Round.

Grab your penis and pull it up (noon position) for 42 seconds

Grab your penis and pull it down (6 o´clock position) for 42 seconds

Grab your penis and pull it to the right (3 o´clock position) for 42 seconds

Grab your penis and pull it to the left (9 o´clock position) for 42 seconds

After finishing the above four motions, grab and stretch the penis from the upwards noon position, and proceed to make a complete circle with your penis while keeping the pulling tension on it at all times.

Perform the circle very slowly. Doing a full circle typically takes anywhere from 40 to 60 seconds. This remains unchanged from the beginner's routine.

Exercise set #2. Basic Penis Stretches. Second-Round.

The second set of stretches in the intermediate program will now target the ligaments by using new angles for a profound effect.

Grab and pull the penis under your legs and behind your glutes backward in the center for 45 seconds.

Grab and pull the penis under your legs and behind your glutes backward to the left for 40 seconds.

Grab and pull the penis under your legs and behind your glutes backward to the left for 40 seconds.

After performing these three motions, it's time to do a full circle, but this time by doing it under your legs, behind your glutes. The circle should last anywhere from 40-60 seconds.

Exercise set #3 Jelqing. Quick reps.

Just as with the intermediate program, jelqs can now be performed with a level 3 erection quality.

Perform 200 repetitions one after another, by using both hands. Each repetition should only last around one second.

Exercise set #4 Jelqing. Slow reps.

Perform 150 repetitions one after another, by using both hands.

Each repetition should last around four seconds.

Exercise #5. The horse squeeze

Perform a single horse squeeze that lasts anywhere from 5 to 10 seconds. With each additional session, add a second to the duration of the exercise until you eventually reach 40 seconds.

Finish the advanced routine by performing the usual cool down. Because of the intensity of the exercises performed, it is a good idea for the cool-down phase to last at least 5 minutes.

CHAPTER 7: SOLIDIFYING YOUR GAINS

One of the most common questions that people ask regarding male enhancement is: will my gains be permanent? The answer is, in most cases, yes. There are some steps that you can take to solidify your gains and significantly increase the likelihood of making them permanent.

The first recommendation is to go beyond your length gains by a small amount. A good rule of thumb is to go for an extra .5" of length or girth to cement your gains. For instance, let's suppose that you currently have an erect length of 6" and your goal is to reach 7.5". In this case, the best way to cement your gains would be to reach 7".

Similar to other types of tissue adaptation and enhancement (such as with muscle building), whenever you stop subjecting the tissue to certain stimulation, there will be a certain degree of reversion.

The great news about male enhancement though, is that gains can easily be permanent by following the extra .5" rule of thumb. With muscle building, for example, it is very easy to lose most of your gains if you completely stop exercising. It is not uncommon for people that have been going religiously to the gym for some time to lose a lot of their gains in just a few months. Penis length and girth gains work differently, and it is very easy to make all the work you've put into it permanent. All you have to do is to shoot for an extra .5," and you'll be good to go.

Do keep in mind that male enhancement exercises have a lot of different benefits besides merely helping you reach a specific size. A lot of men might be able to reach their size goals relatively quickly but might choose to remain on a male enhancement routine.

Better libido, firmer erections, and improved ejaculation control are all great benefits of a solid male enhancement routine. Don't be afraid to go back to the exercises whenever you'd like to enjoy a boost in your sex life. When done in a responsible fashion and with proper recovery periods, you can perform male enhancement exercises almost indefinitely.

CHAPTER 8: COMMONLY ASKED QUESTIONS ABOUT MALE ENHANCEMENT

Male enhancement is undoubtedly taboo in most cultures and can even be subject to ridicule from people that don't understand what it is all about. As with any taboo topic, there are a lot of questions surrounding it. We will try to cover the most common of them in this chapter so that you have a broader understanding of the topic.

Q. Why would I want to increase the size of my penis?

A. Increasing the size of your penis is entirely up to you. No one is telling you that you should have a bigger penis size. You might have a smaller than average penis size, but if in the end you feel happy about it and it doesn't bother you or cause any self-esteem issues, then there is little reason to increase the size of your penis.

However, a lot of men from most cultures aren't satisfied with their current penis size and would love to have a longer or thicker sex organ because this is typically a very desirable attribute. Women from most cultures would rather have a man with a bigger penis than a smaller one if they had to choose. However, as you probably know by now, a lot of women are satisfied with the penis size of their partners and have a very different idea of what a big penis is.

If you've always wanted to be bigger than you currently are, then, by all means, you should go for it. There is no denying that eventually achieving a bigger size will have a very positive impact on your life. Men that have successfully managed to grow their penises through male enhancement programs or devices tend to mention that it was one of the best decisions they ever made, as their sense of self-confidence becomes much increased, not only inside the bedroom but in many other areas of their life. They also tend to enjoy sex more, as their new confidence helps reduce performance anxiety if there ever was any. Partners also tend to be unexpectedly surprised and enjoy having sex more, although there are some exceptions; in some cases, men may go too far with their enhancement goals and reach a size that becomes too uncomfortable for their partners.

If you currently are in a relationship or are having sex with someone you have good communication with, you should talk with your partner before starting any male enhancement routine. If it is a partner that you care about, then their opinion will be important to you. Sometimes you might be surprised to hear that they are completely satisfied with your current size and might not like the idea of you having a bigger penis, as it may prove to be uncomfortable for them. However, if it's important to you, tell them about the benefits that male enhancement will give you, as it is very likely that your self-confidence will change after going through a program if you're currently not satisfied with your size.

Q: How do these manual male enhancement exercises work? It can be hard to believe that one can quickly increase the size of their genitals with just their bare hands.

A: It is surprisingly simple to explain. Whenever you expose the tissue of your penis to progressive resistance, you will create micro-tears in it. A somewhat similar process happens when you exercise your muscles. After these micro-tears appear, your body gets the message that it's crucial to adapt to this new stress or something terrible might happen. In other words, the body is forced to change in an "adapt or die" fashion.

You leave it with little choice.

The body then tries to repair the micro-tears you have created by repairing them, making the tissues stronger, and promoting growth.

Q: What is the best way to know that I'm right on track?

A: As mentioned previously, each individual is different regarding how their body lets them know that they are making progress. However, for most people, the first positive sign of progress with most male enhancement exercises and even with the use of some devices will be an improvement in erection quality. If there is a noticeable improvement in the firmness and strength of your erections, then this is a good sign that you should continue to do what you've been doing so far. What tends to follow shortly after this is visible size increments.

However, keep in mind that these initial increments tend to be short term only. It is also very common to notice that the penis has become slightly larger or thicker after performing a male enhancement routine.

If you keep doing the same exercises that are stimulating your tissues positively, eventually, these short term size gains will become permanent.

Q: I don't enjoy warming up before doing the exercises, is it ok if I skip the warm-up step?

A: Some men will be able to skip the warm-up and still manage to avoid issues such as discomfort, overtraining, pain, etc. But as general advice, avoid skipping warm-up as much as possible. Even if you do ok with skipping warm-up, and the gains continue, it may be only a matter of time until overtraining, or pain catches up to you. What warming up helps with is preparing your penis for more intense exercise by increasing blood flow into that area in a very gentle way.

Q: I'm afraid of injuring myself while doing some of the male enhancement exercises. What is the worst that can happen?

A: We only recommend starting the male enhancement routines here after consulting with a physician first.

Keep in mind that every individual is different and will respond differently to male enhancement, but as a general rule of thumb, it is never ok to experience pain while doing the exercises. As mentioned, we should forget about the "no pain, no gain" rule with male enhancement. We are dealing with delicate tissue, and as such, it is essential to pay close attention to what our bodies are telling us. Sometimes, using excessive frequency or intensity that your body isn't able to tolerate will end up causing setbacks.

Here are some of the most common signs that you need to back off and give your body a break to recover before continuing with any male enhancement exercises:

-Any time of recurring pain in the genital area.

-Feeling as though the penis is exhausted.

-Loss of erection quality.

-Vein thrombosis.

-Loss of sexual desire.

-In some of the more severe cases, short term erectile dysfunction.

Q: I'm not sure if I'm pulling with the right amount of force when I'm doing manual stretches.

A: There is no standard answer to this because different men feel different things when performing manual stretches. However, the most common sensation reported is that of a slight sense of tingling or itchiness along the penis shaft. Please be careful and exercise smartly. A tingling sensation is very different to feeling pain if you feel pain at any time, back off with the force or intensity.

Q: Do I need to follow a male enhancement program? Can't I do the exercises I want whenever I want?

A: While it is definitively not required to follow a program to make size gains, I recommend sticking to one because it is most likely the quickest and easiest way to reach your size goals. When you decide not to follow a program and do exercises at random, it is much more likely for you to over train and encounter many bumps in the road that will significantly slow down your progress. The programs have been designed to take you from point a to point b with as minimal amount of setbacks as possible.

In the end, whether you follow a program or not is entirely up to you. If you decide not to follow a program and you instead would like to perform exercises any time you'd like to, we recommend always listening to what your body is telling you. A lot of men have made some great size gains without following a program, but the key to their success has always been listening to their bodies. Once you have some experience, you will be better able to know when you are about to stumble on overtraining or a setback that will hinder your advance. At the beginning stages, you will probably see the best gains possible if you decide to stick with a program.

Q: Is it ok if I modify my current program? Can I add a particular exercise to it?

A: The answer will be similar to the previous one. Some people might get away with adding new exercises to their current routine or not following a problem, but it may not always work. Programs usually have an exercise selection that tends to work great together and has a very high ratio of success. They are also designed to help you avoid as many setbacks as possible. Many times, the exercises in a program interact well with one another and will help you hit your penis from diverse angles for optimal growth. If you wish to experiment (although we don't recommend it), you can add an exercise to your program and see how your body responds. If you stop seeing positive signs, then it's better to return to a previous point where you were making progress.

Q: I got interested in male enhancement devices after reading about them. Is it ok if I add a specific device to my current program?

A: Adding a device such as a water-based pump or a penis extender to your current program means that you will be adding additional stress to your body.

As said before, you might get away with it, but it's always best to listen to what your body is telling you. We can't stress this point enough.

Q: Will male enhancement exercises help me if I have issues such as weak erections, erectile dysfunction, or low libido.

A: In most cases, male enhancement exercises will help with a lot of the typical male sex problems. These exercises tend to promote blood flow inside the penis tissue and promote overall penis health. Some of the earliest signs of progress are improved erections. Some men have found that male enhancement exercises have been all they need to improve their male sex issues. Performing Kegels, for instance, is a great way to improve premature ejaculation, by strengthening your pelvic floor muscles. However, in many cases, male enhancement exercises won't be enough.

Some male sex issues such as erectile dysfunction may be a sign of a more complex health problem, such as atherosclerosis or diabetes, so it's best to check yourself with a physician first.

Q: I'm afraid of causing long term damage to my penis by doing the exercises.

A: When performed as recommended, the exercises included in this guide are perfectly safe and should pose no harm to your health. You'd have to not listen to your body and continue to press on regardless of the pain for a while to cause any long term damage.

Some of the exercises that you have to be careful with are manual stretches, as it is very easy to apply too much force when doing them. As you now know, short term effects are typically a loss of libido and worse erection quality, but fortunately, these tend to last only a few days and get better with a few rest days. Using a little common sense will pay dividends with male enhancement. If it hurts, then you shouldn't be doing it. Plain and simple.

Q: Realistically, how many inches can I expect to gain when following the programs included in this guide?

A: One of the objectives of this book is to give you a realistic way to achieve your penis size goals while informing you of the most common frauds in the male enhancement industry.

Realistically, you can expect to increase your penis for at least 2-3 inches if you follow the program.

As with anything health-related, the results may significantly vary with each individual. There are some men that have an easy time gaining more inches after the initial 2-3 inches gained. Some have reported incredible gains, up to 5 inches or more gained, but this is definitively uncommon.

Considering that even a single inch can make a drastic difference in your confidence and sex life, 2-3 inches sounds like a pretty good deal!

Q: Are there any supplements that will help me see quicker gains when following the male enhancement programs?

A: Supplements are entirely optional. Some supplements are known for giving a significant boost to the libido, erection quality, and overall penile health. However, there is no reliable research done yet that has proven that supplements can help improve the results of male enhancement.

As always, don't forget to consult with your physician before including supplements to your diet. Some of the supplements we can recommend for overall male sexual health are:

-Omega 3 supplements. The most common of which are fish oil capsules, but there are many different options, such as supplements derived from algae or flaxseed. There has been a lot of research that suggests that Omega 3 supplements are one of the best supplements that humans can take because of the countless benefits they offer to our health. Omega 3 supplements have been reported to improve libido and erection quality in a lot of men. However, there have been some rare cases where they cause the contrary effect, so in the end, it is best to always listen to your body.

-Ginseng. People have been using this plant for millennia, and its use is still widespread in our current times. You are probably already familiar with this ginseng, since there are lots of different products on sale at your average drugstore that contains it: teas, pills, powders, candies, etc. It has been popularly used to treat some male sex issues such as erectile dysfunction and stamina loss. Some claim that it also improved libido for them. The great thing about ginseng is that it's available in many forms and has very little reported side effects.

-Zinc. An essential trace mineral that we all need in adequate amounts to feel healthy; it is only second to iron in its concentration in the human body. Having a zinc deficiency may cause lots of different health issues such as appetite loss, hair loss, bowel problems, and impotence. It can also impair immune function. It has been linked with male health by a lot of medical evidence. Although some argue their effectiveness, zinc supplements can be beneficial with libido and stamina. Some men have reported that zinc supplements have increased the size of their ejaculations. Zinc may give some side effects, so it's best to always check via blood testing if your levels are not over the range.

-Epimedium. You'll find this plant as a supplement in pill form, and it is often called "horny goat weed." The positive effects reported by those that consume epimedium are an increase in libido, stamina, and an improvement in erectile dysfunction or erection quality in some cases. Results can be very different from individual to individual (although this warning probably applies to every supplement mentioned in this list), and while there have been many cases of success, there have also been lots of men that have reported noticing no effect at all. Epimedium needs to be consumed for a while to receive its benefits. Some may notice the effects after the second or third week.

-Vitamin E. While there is little evidence that vitamin E can be beneficial for overall male sexual health, it can be an excellent supplement for men with Peyronie's disease. This disease is a condition where the penis has an abnormal curve when erect. This condition is usually connected to scar tissue or plaque located inside the penis. For some men, this can be a challenging condition to manage because it causes great pain whenever the penis becomes erect. There is research that supports the use of vitamin e as a way to improve the painful effects of this disease with little side effects. Because there is no current cure for this disease, vitamin E can make a big difference for some men.

-Vitamin D. One of the most common vitamin to be deficient in, Vitamin D is linked to a host of different issues related to poor male sexual health, the most common being erectile dysfunction. It is one of the most hotly debated vitamins, but there is some evidence that it is probably linked to elevated levels of higher testosterone and overall better male sexual health. Besides the male sex benefits, vitamin D is crucial for reducing cardiovascular risk, protecting our body from certain cancers, and protecting endothelial cells from oxidative stress.

CHAPTER 9: HOW TO OVERCOME PREMATURE EJACULATION

One of the most common problems for males in the bedroom is premature ejaculation. If you are currently suffering from this issue, rest assured that your condition is not unique. A lot of men suffer from premature ejaculation. Around 20 percent of men may suffer from premature ejaculation at some point during their lives, although the issue might be minor in most cases to become a real problem.

Younger men are the ones that suffer from premature ejaculation the most, but this is an issue that can affect men from pretty much every age. It can cause a huge dent in the self-esteem and confidence of men.

In some severe cases, it can even cause some difficult psychological issues, and it may also affect relationships.

So what is premature ejaculation, and why does it happen? When a man ejaculates too soon for his partner to achieve orgasm or enjoy sex on multiple occasions, we can confidently say that he's suffering from premature ejaculation.

For the issue to be considered premature ejaculation, the duration might vary from culture to culture, but typically lasting anywhere from less than 30 seconds to 4 minutes is commonly an issue.

In some cases, premature ejaculation might be such a problem that the man ejaculates soon after penetration starts. Some men might even ejaculate without initiating penetration, and physical contact from his contact might be enough to cause him an orgasm.

Men that are deeply aware of their premature ejaculation problem tend to suffer from anxiety issues before, during, and after sexual activity.

Such anxiety tends to further affect their performance during sex or even worsen the problem in some cases as being relaxed is usually one of the requirements of having reasonable ejaculation control.

There's two different main types of premature ejaculation identified by experts: lifelong and acquired or secondary premature ejaculation.

This issue can be sometimes tricky to treat because it usually is linked to more complex psychological problems that have to be addressed to treat it successfully. Bad habits are sometimes the cause of premature ejaculation. During puberty or adolescence, some boys tend to have masturbation habits that hinder their performance later during sexual intercourse.

The most common of these habits is trying to reach orgasm as quickly as possible. Patterns during adolescence may carry over to adulthood if they're not addressed.

Acquired or secondary premature ejaculation tends to happen at the later stages of a man's life. Sometimes, psychological issues can be deeply rooted and difficult to treat. If a man has a bad sexual experience during his first sexual contact (which might have happened during adolescence), this might continue to haunt him and affect his performance until it is properly addressed.

Certain health conditions might cause premature ejaculation, such as having high blood pressure, diabetes, or hormonal disbalances.

For some lucky few, premature ejaculation can get much better on its own.

For men that aren't used to sexual contact with a partner, the issue might simply improve by having more practice and getting used to the new sensations.

Male enhancement exercises such as those included in this guide can work wonders for some cases of premature ejaculation. Exercises such as Kegels and even manual stretching can give them better control of the muscles that give them better ejaculation control. However, in some cases, this won't be enough, and other solutions need to have to be considered.

Also, for a lot of men, it is possible to improve their premature ejaculation problem after doing some simple lifestyle changes. For instance, drastically cutting down tobacco or alcohol intake, plus eating a better diet can alleviate a lot of the anxiety that plagues men during sexual intercourse, which in itself might be an active contributor to their premature ejaculation problem. Having excess levels of stress can significantly hinder a man's performance in bed.

There are also a few short-term fixes that can be very useful in a pinch.

For instance, it is now very easy to buy special condoms that include substances that decrease the sensitivity in the penis. These substances are also sold by themselves, usually as creams or sprays. These products typically include lidocaine or lidocaine-prilocaine, very common and safe numbing substances. Wearing a thicker condom can also be a straightforward way to decrease sensitivity. The main side effect of these options is that there will be some reduction in pleasure, and sometimes, erection quality might also suffer as a direct consequence of this.

Arguably, the best recommendation for men that are suffering from this issue is to perform exercises that improve their ejaculation control. Similar to male enhancement exercises, they can be a very convenient solution that can be practiced anywhere while being completely free.

A lot of sex experts recommend Kegels as an exercise to improve ejaculation control, but since we've already looked at them in great detail in previous chapters, there is no need to go over them again.

Here are some other exercises that have proven to be invaluable to a lot of men suffering from premature ejaculation.

Edging or the "Stop-Start" technique

Edging is one of the best ways to practice ejaculation control without the need of having actual sexual intercourse. This technique can be done both by yourself or with a partner, but we highly recommend that you practice it by yourself with masturbation first. The reason why is because it can be very stressful on your partner to be always stopping sexual penetration, which is something you'll need to do.

To practice edging, you start by masturbating as you usually would, but you stop before you begin to feel as though you are about to ejaculate. The best way to avoid ejaculating is by using a scale of 1 to 10 or 1 to 100 to rank your current level of stimulation. One means barely aroused while 10 or 100 means that you've reached the point of no return and you are about to ejaculate.

When you practice edging, it's essential to be conscious of where your current level of stimulation is at and to never go past a 7 or an 8 (or 70, 80, if you're using a 1-100 scale). Once you reach a 9 in stimulation, it is tough to go back, and you will probably go the full way and end up finishing. If you feel that you are reaching a level 8, stop and take a few deep breaths. Let your level of arousal go back to at least a 4 or a 5 before continuing. Going back to a previous level of arousal might sometimes take 30-40 seconds or more.

Mixing oral or manual stimulation

While this is not a strategy to cure premature ejaculation, it does help in a pinch if you ever feel like you are reaching the point of no return while having sexual intercourse. Whenever you're having sex, you can apply edging, but whenever you notice that you've reached the point where you need to back off, instead of completely stopping all sexual activity, stop penetration, but continue to pleasure your partner by using manual or oral stimulation. Stimulating them with your hands or mouth will take care of most of the drawbacks of using edging while having sexual intercourse.

The squeeze strategy

Just as the name implies, the squeeze technique is done by simply squeezing your penis in the area right between the shaft and the glans.

In most cases, doing this will help you go back to a previous level of stimulation and stop the ejaculation. It can be a potent tool to stop your orgasms from happening, but in some instances, where you are dangerously near the point of no return, it won't be enough to stop the ejaculation. It is up to you to experiment and see at which point of stimulation it remains to be an effective means of stopping ejaculation.

This technique, while great, isn't recommended to be used more than three to five times during each session, as it can affect erection quality and reduce your sensitivity.

Having sex more often

Merely having more sex might sound like obvious advice, but don't underestimate the effectiveness of it; by simply having more sex, you will get used to the sensations and become less stimulated when having intercourse or getting touched by your partner. You will also gain better control of your body and mind and will help you relax more and enjoy what's going on.

Sex Toys

While sex toys are more commonly used by females, there are a lot of great male sex toys available, and a lot of them can be an excellent option for practicing ejaculation control. They are also an excellent option for men that currently do not have a partner, as they can give levels of stimulation that are beyond what the hands can provide via typical masturbation.

Some male sex toys are designed to feel like a vagina. They stimulate the sensations that a real vagina gives to a penis so that you can practice edging and other techniques to improve your control.

Ejaculating before having sex

Ejaculating before sexual intercourse is one of the most common pieces of advice given to men with ejaculation control problems. If you masturbate and reach orgasm one or two hours before having sexual intercourse, your penis won't feel as sensitive as before. The decreased stimulation from the orgasm that you recently reached will give you extra time when having sexual stimulation. The opposite tends to happen when there has been a prolonged period between orgasms; your penis will be highly sensitive, and it is more likely that you will reach orgasms faster.

Masturbating frequently is a great way to reduce the sensitivity of the penis without having to use a numbing agent or a thicker condom. However, this might not work for men that aren't able to achieve a firm erection after ejaculating. So only perform this technique if you are sure that you can achieve a firm erection an hour or two after ejaculating, as you don't want to be in a situation where you aren't able to perform.

Distracting the mind

Distracting the mind can be a potent trick for ejaculation control. It is also another one of those techniques that men with premature ejaculation issues should use. Whenever you feel like you are being stimulated and feel that you are reaching the point of no return, you can try thinking about people or things that you find entirely disgusting.

While this method can be very effective, a lot of people argue that it shouldn't be used because it greatly decreases the overall enjoyment you'll get out of having sex. You can try using it sparingly after trying some of the other methods.

Taking deep breaths

Premature ejaculation is often a result of anxiety. A lot of men with great control during sex can hold off their ejaculation for prolonged periods thanks to their ability to remain relaxed. Once specific pelvic muscles become contracted and tense, it is very easy to reach the point of no return.

To relax our bodies, it all begins with our breathing. If you're not sure how to start, try to inhale through your nose and exhale through your mouth after three to four seconds. Taking deep breaths will do wonders to calm down and relax the mind and the body.

Deep breaths improve blood oxygenation (SpO2), which then help your brain release more endorphins. More endorphins mean that you'll feel overall happier and more relaxed during sex.

Communicating with your partner

For some men, premature ejaculation is directly caused by anxiety issues. Sometimes, the best way to relax and calm down anxiety levels is by simply communicating with your partner and being honest about the situation. It can be beneficial to talk about your worries during sex. Talking honestly with your partner can significantly relieve pressure and increase your bond.

In some more complicated cases, talking to a therapist might be necessary, as some men have deeply rooted self-image issues or a history of problems that might be contributing to the premature ejaculation.

Sometimes only a professional can uncover the underlying issues that may be causing damage.

Pills

Some men with very severe premature ejaculation issues might try several of the methods mentioned and find little to no success with them. If you've tried several natural methods and find that the problem persists, then you can talk to your physician about the issue so that he may prescribe you pills.

If psychological issues or mood disorders such as anxiety or depression are what's causing poor ejaculation control, then some doctors might prescribe medication to improve those disorders. Meds can be a good option for men that have already exhausted a lot of different options.

CHAPTER 10: Overcoming erectile DYSFUNCTION

The number one male sex problem reported is not premature ejaculation, but erectile dysfunction. It is a very common experience that fortunately, can be reversed in many cases.

So what is exactly erectile dysfunction? ED is when there is a considerable difficulty of getting or keeping an erection that is firm enough to have regular sexual intercourse. It is very common for men to experience minor issues getting a firm erection from time to time, but when the problem worsens with time or happens consistently when sex is about to happen, it becomes a significant issue.

There can be several causes for ED. The most common of them are stress and emotional or psychological reasons. Other physical causes include restricted blood flow in the penis, such as when nerves are limited or damaged. ED can also be an early sign of a severe health issue such as atherosclerosis, heart disease, or high blood sugar.

How do erections work?

When there is enough sexual arousal, the nerves release chemicals that start increasing blood flow into the penis tissue. This blood starts to flow into the two erection chambers located inside the penis, which made of spongy muscle tissue. This spongy tissue tends to relax to trap blood during an erection. The blood pressure in the erection chambers makes the penis to become firm enough to have regular sexual intercourse.

When a man reaches orgasm, other nerves are in charge of signaling to the penis to contract to release the blood back to the man's circulation, and as a result, the erection comes down.

When a man is nor sexually aroused, the normal of the penis is to be soft and limp. The size of the penis can vary a lot depending on different factors such as the weather (cold weather tends to temporarily decrease penis size, while warm weather may increase it) and mood. This is completely normal and shouldn't be a cause for worrying.

As mentioned, real erectile dysfunction happens when a male has difficulty to keep an erection that is firm enough to have regular sexual intercourse with his partner.

Some of the typical physical causes of ed tend to be the following:

-Being 50 years or older.

-Certain diseases and conditions, such as diabetes or high blood pressure.

-Substantial consumption of alcohol, smoking, or other drugs.

-Little exercise

-Being obese or overweight.

While it is true that aging increases the likelihood of getting ED, growing old doesn't mean that you will automatically get ED, a lot of men are capable of having firm erections in their 70's or 80's.

Some of the most common emotional or psychological causes of ED are:

-Mood disorders or mood-altering events such as depression, stress, and anxiety.

-Relationship problems.

-Worrying about sexual performance.

Can erectile dysfunction be reversed?

The good news is that yes, in many cases, ED can definitively be reversed. Even in situations when the ED can't be changed, the correct treatment can do wonders to greatly reduce the symptoms.

There have been two identified types of this condition:

-Primary Erectile dysfunction. Happens when a man has never been able to produce a firm erection in his life. Fortunately, this is an extremely rare condition.

-Secondary erectile dysfunction. Men that were previously able to sustain firm erections but are no longer capable have this type of ED. This one is the more common of the two.

Secondary erectile dysfunction is often more easily treated than primary and usually is only temporary. Primary erectile dysfunction needs more intensive care and specialized medical products or surgery in some cases.

In some cases of secondary erectile dysfunction, it can be reversible without having to use drugs by treating the underlying causes.

Treating ED

There are several different treatments for ED, and they vary depending on each individual's needs. Some men might have a lot of success by simply changing their lifestyle, while for others, the only thing that will work is medication or surgery. Fortunately, ED is often easily treated without having to resort to drugs or complicated procedures.

There are short term treatments that can dramatically improve erections, but unfortunately, do little to address the real cause of ED. Certain drugs available in the market can significantly increase blood flow to the penis, and provide temporary relief from ED.

These drugs are typically used by males of ages 50 and up. However, it is common for physicians to prescribe them to younger patients if they believe that it will improve their quality of life. Some people with specific conditions such as atherosclerosis or diabetes can significantly benefit from these medications too.

In some cases, it is possible to treat the primary cause of erectile dysfunction and reverse the condition. For instance, if clogged arteries are restricting blood flow inside the penis, then losing weight, exercising, or taking medication to address this issue will undoubtedly impact erection quality.

Just like with other male-bedroom related issues, low testosterone often causes ED. Whenever there are male-bedroom related issues going on, one of the most recommended and easiest things to do is to get testosterone levels properly checked to have a more accurate picture of what's going on.

In some instances, the cause of erectile dysfunction can be psychological or emotional. We'll see how this tends to happen later in this chapter.

As mentioned previously, making lifestyle adjustments can sometimes be all you need to do to reverse erectile dysfunction. Eating a healthier diet, exercising, losing weight when necessary, and reducing one's intake of alcohol and tobacco can sometimes do the trick.

In some cases, specific exercises can be extremely helpful to treat reduced blood flow inside the penis. Many of the exercises in this guide will be particularly useful for this purpose. When performing the male enhancement routines correctly, you'll probably start noticing firmer and stronger erections. Improvement in erection quality is one of the precursors of making long-lasting gains with male enhancement exercises or devices. Certain exercise such as Kegels can be particularly useful for improving and retaining blood flow inside the penis.

Just as with other male bedroom issues, certain medications can have unwanted side effects that can affect erection quality or testosterone production. In such cases, talking to your physician and asking about other similar drugs without these side effects can be a good idea. Often, there are alternative drugs available that won't have the side effects that affect performance in the bedroom.

The connection between anxiety and ED

One of the most common causes of ED is anxiety. There is even a name to identify the erectile dysfunction caused by it: performance anxiety. Whenever a man feels very stressed about his performance in the bedroom, it can easily lead to erectile dysfunction.

Men tend to feel very self-conscious about their performance in the bedroom, and sometimes their partners or themselves place high expectations that end up worrying and causing unnecessary stress that ends up leading to ED.

Whenever a man feels like he is not able to perform to his sexual expectations, then it can easily lead to a vicious downward spiral of negative feelings and emotions such as low self-esteem or feelings of inadequacy.

What tends to cause performance anxiety?

There can be several things that eventually lead to performance anxiety. As previously mentioned, it can be caused by having negative thoughts about their ability to perform well in the bedroom and to please their partner.

Several can directly influence these feelings: such as their self-esteem, size of their penis, or their perceptions about what it means to be a man in the bedroom. A man's mental state can also influence and contribute to their performance anxiety. For instance, if they've been having a lot of problems at work, or with their family, these can eventually contribute to their performance in the bedroom.

Performance anxiety can manifest itself in many ways, as everyone responds differently to stress and anxiety. While it is most often connected to erectile dysfunction, it can also produce other issues such as premature ejaculation, low sexual appetite, or having a difficult time achieving ejaculation.

Dealing with performance anxiety

While it may sound obvious, the best thing you can do is to prevent falling into the cycle.

Getting trapped in the cycle can be very hard to deal with, so it's best if one can avoid falling into the trap in the first place.

Whenever a man has a disappointing sexual experience (for instance, he may have ejaculated too quickly or was unable to give his partner an orgasm), he might start to dwell on this event and begin to feel like he is a failure in the bedroom. Having a disappointing sexual experience from time to time is nothing to be worried about, as it is entirely normal.

The problem arises when men can't stop dwelling on his bedroom failure, which eventually leads them to start feeling anxious about how they will perform next time. This is the cycle that causes erectile dysfunction to continue.

Whenever you don't perform as you or your partner expect in the bedroom, you should understand that what happened is a perfectly normal event. Instead of obsessing about the negative event that happened, use your focus and energy on trying to identify what happened and how you can improve next time. You might have been overly stressed due to something that happened at work or with your family/friends. If such is the case, then try to think about ways how you could solve that issue so that the worry and stress don't spill over to other areas of your life.

Another piece of solid advice for men who experience performance anxiety is to shift their focus to their senses. After all, worry and anxiety are primarily caused by our thoughts. If most of our attention and focus is on our senses, then there is little opportunity for anxiety to creep up.

During bedroom activity, the best you can do, regardless of whether you have performance anxiety or not, is to focus on your senses instead of being inside your head analyzing what's happening. Put your attention on what your hands and skin are feeling and on what your eyes are seeing so that you can block anxious thoughts. Another way to prevent negative thoughts is to use calming music and sensual aromas to help your senses.

It can also be beneficial to talk with your partner about the anxiety you are experiencing. The simple act of opening up and talking your worries will help you feel less stressed. Once your partner knows about this issue, you can both then find solutions to help improve the situation. Couples counseling or sex therapy can also be a great idea that will help both of you get on the right track again.

If none of this works, then it might be time to visit a doctor. Anyone that continues to experience erectile dysfunction even after they've tried a few solutions can benefit from talking to a doctor about their physical or physiological symptoms.

CHAPTER 11: REVERSING LOW LIBIDO

It's now time to tackle another common bedroom issue that plagues a lot of men: low libido or low sexual desire.

First of all, it's important to mention that people have varying degrees of sexual desire. Sexual appetite is impossible to standardize as it continually changes throughout a person's life. A man's libido in his late 40's will look very different from what it was during his teenage years.

A prevalent complaint among partners is a disparity in sexual appetite. Sexual appetite can be very different for multiple different reasons outside of age; for instance, factors such as the mental and physical health of a person plays an important role.

For example, your sexual appetite could be affected for a short period, but this doesn't necessarily mean that you're suffering from a disorder. It becomes an issue when it starts diminishing the quality of life of the person and creates a lot of unnecessary stress on him and/or his partner. It is not unusual for low libido to cause a lot of problems in relationships and marriages.

Also, the condition of low libido can be very relative. Partners inside a relationship tend to think of the sexual appetite experienced early on in a relationship as the standard to judge their sexual desire during the rest of their partnership, but this shouldn't be the case since there will always be a natural drop of sexual appetite after some time during any relationship. Also, a person with a naturally high libido might think that his partner is experiencing low sexual drive, while in reality, they are the ones with the unusual "hyperactive" sex drive.

It's also important to mention that sexual drive and responsiveness tends to be very different among males and females. Members of one sex might wrongly think that the other sex should have a similar level of sexual desire as them, while in reality, it's much easier for a male to become more easily aroused on a physical level than females. For males, sexual desire is deeply connected to physical arousal. On the other hand, females tend to have a more complex sex drive that is more tied to their psychological and situational states than their physical. The way they feel about their bodies and their partners has a profound influence on their sexual desire. Also, females tend to only experience biological sexual desire until there has been some degree of genital arousal. Such a concept can be tough to comprehend for males, who can be instantly turned on after seeing a picture of a female they feel sexually attracted.

How to recognize a real low libido problem

So the question is, how can we recognize when there truly is a situation of low sex desire? What constitutes a healthy level of sexual appetite can be highly dependent upon each individual. It is normal to have a lower sexual desire at specific points of our lives; for instance, when we are going through a difficult situation that spikes our stress levels up, our sexual appetite will probably lower. Higher levels of the stress hormone cortisol in our system tend to wreak havoc in many of our body's functions, and our sex drive is no exception.

The classification and study of problems related to low libido have been studied by researchers and clinicians for a while now. The most common symptoms of low libido that usually present themselves as an evident lack of response to a partner's normal sexual behavior include:

-Having difficulty getting sexually aroused

-A generally low level of baseline sexual interest

-Lack of sexual dreams

-Having thoughts that affect sexual performance.

-It may or may not include erectile dysfunction.

The most common physical causes of these symptoms include fluctuations in endocrine hormones. For instance, men that tend to have low testosterone will almost always experience a decrease in their sexual desire. On the other hand, women that are experiencing lower levels of estrogen tend to also suffer from a decrease in sexual appetite.

Probably the most common psychological factor is depression.

Some antidepressant drugs tend to have cause low libido as a side effect. Other conditions such as fatigue, poor self-esteem, and a history of sexual abuse can also affect a person's level of sexual desire.

Relationship problems such as lack of trust, having unresolved conflict and lack of communication can also reduce sexual desire, although this is most commonly seen affecting more females than males. However, resentment in a relationship can be a significant cause of libido loss, and this is something that affects both men and women equally.

How to treat low libido

The great news is that if you are currently doing a male enhancement routine, such as those included in this guide, your levels of sexual arousal are very likely to increase. This improvement happens primarily due to the increased flow of blood in the genital region.

However, in many cases, this won't be enough to deal with a severe issue of low sexual desire.

The pressure of being instantly ready to have sex can be an issue for a lot of men, and make coping with lost libido even more difficult. If so, then communicating with your partner to let them know that your libido issues aren't because of her should be one of your priorities. In some cases, talking to a sex therapist will do a world of good to improve the situation.

For men, the number one cause of low libido issues is a drop in testosterone levels. Successfully treating any condition begins by making the right diagnosis. If you're a man that's currently experiencing a decrease in sexual appetite, the best course of action is probably to start by getting your testosterone levels checked. A simple blood test will be enough to confirm if you are having this issue or not. If you are checking your testosterone levels, it is best to check them in the morning, as test levels tend to be the highest during this time.

There are varying degrees of low testosterone. Sometimes, straightforward lifestyle changes can result in a sufficient boost of male hormone production, and if levels aren't too low, this might be enough to do the trick. We recommend the following basic lifestyle changes if your testosterone levels are slightly on the low side:

-Exercising. Getting enough moderate exercise every week should do wonders to your testosterone levels. Don't overwork yourself, as this can quickly fatigue you and worsen the problem. Around 200 minutes of moderate exercise every week is recommended, although the duration and intensity tolerance depends from person to person.

-Losing weight. People that are overweight or obese tend to experience lower levels of testosterone, according to some studies. Lowering your levels of abdominal fat usually equals to an improvement in libido.

-Get your diet in check. A diet that is high in junk food and low in fruits, vegetables, and omega fatty acids tend to cause a drop in testosterone levels. Try to cut out as much junk food as possible from your diet, and increase your intake of fruits and vegetables along with foods that are high in Omega 3's, (such as walnuts, salmon, sardines, etc.).

-Check your medications. Check if you are currently taking any medications that might have adverse effects on testosterone levels. If you find anything that might be having a negative impact, you can talk to your physician and check if it's possible to switch medications to something that has fewer side effects on your t levels.

-Alcohol, smoking, and other drugs. Significant consumption of alcohol and tobacco have been shown to influence why some men have lower levels of testosterone. The same applies to other illegal substances. Decreasing the use of these substances or quitting might improve libido.

-Therapy. If you are going through a stressful event during your life, your high cortisol levels are probably contributing to your decreased testosterone levels. If you are currently experiencing high levels of stress, talking to a therapist or a close friend will help you cope with the situation, or at least find temporary relief until the case hopefully improves.

It is also very typical to have a decreased level of testosterone with aging. T levels will typically peak during adolescence. There is a point in every male's life where testosterone starts to slowly decline (usually after age 30 or 40). Fortunately, with the above lifestyle changes, it is possible to improve the effects that aging has on the male hormone.

If your testosterone levels are low enough, then your physician, typically an endocrinologist, will usually suggest testosterone replacement therapy. Your testosterone will probably be tested twice before the suggestion for replacement therapy is made.

Currently, physicians suggest testosterone replacement therapy primarily when there is a medical condition (such as hypogonadism, where the body is unable to produce sufficient testosterone due to an issue in the testicles) that is causing an unusual decline in testosterone. Some clinicians will not suggest testosterone replacement therapy when the decrease in testosterone is due to normal aging; however, some of them are more open-minded about the subject and might give you options if this is your case. A certified clinician will be able to tell you the potential pros and cons of testosterone replacement therapy, in case that it is an option at your disposal.

CHAPTER 12: WHAT TO DO ABOUT DELAYED OR INHIBITED EJACULATION

Delayed or inhibited ejaculation might not be at the top of the list of male sexual disorders, but in reality, it can be just as frustrating or even more so than premature ejaculation in some cases.

Some men that have a hard time prolonging their ejaculation, or those that are currently suffering from premature ejaculation might think that having delayed ejaculation could be a nice problem to have, but the truth is that it can cause a lot of damage in a relationship.

So what exactly is delayed inhibited ejaculation? Just as the name implies, it is the inability to reach climax while having sexual intercourse.

A lot of the times, men with this problem may be able to reach orgasm with masturbation, but not during vaginal penetration. The inability to orgasm while inside your partner can be frustrating for both the man and his partner. Partners of men with this issue sometimes wonder if they are the cause of this issue, by not being attractive enough to them or not being able to please them as expected.

It is considered to be the third most common male sexual issue, with the first two being impotence and premature ejaculation. Probably as a consequence of this, it hasn't been as studied as the other two male sexual disorders, and there is very little medical literature on it. It is also not as easy to treat as the other male sexual disorders.

What are the causes of inhibited or delayed ejaculation?

Most researchers on the subject agree that the primary cause of inhibited or delayed ejaculation is psychological. Most men that suffer from this issue tend to be extremely controlled in most areas of their lives, or have had a very strict upbringing.

It is also prevalent in men that are high performance or overachievers in their professions.

Men that tend to have a lot of discipline and control directed inward instead than at others tend to be the ones that suffer from this issue the most.

Some other factors can also cause men to have delayed ejaculation, such as the fear of getting their partner pregnant, masturbating too much, or having a very strict upbringing.

Men that are heavily conditioned by their masturbation habits have a tough time getting enough stimulation from a woman's vagina to reach ejaculation.

There are also other causes of delayed ejaculation. For instance, most men find it harder to reach orgasm as they age. There might be a lot of different reasons for this. Having less testosterone means that the sensations felt in the penis will be less intense than what they were before. One of the first things reported by patients that have undergone testosterone replacement therapy successfully is the increased pleasurable sensations in the penis during sexual activity.

Just as with the other male sexual issues, some drugs can have side effects that influence the ability to reach orgasm.

Although rarer, there are some spinal injuries can also cause significant problems when trying to achieve an orgasm.

Common problems caused by delayed ejaculation

As mentioned previously, a lot of men that have a problematic time prolonging their ejaculation might find it hard to believe that a delayed ejaculation might cause issues during sexual intercourse. However, it can indeed cause a lot of self-esteem and inadequacy problems, not only in the man but with his partner as well. The partner might start feeling inadequate and find sexual activity less enjoyable than what it was before.

In a strong and supportive relationship, delayed ejaculation shouldn't be an issue at all. As with any other matters in a relationship, it's best to keep your partner involved at all times and to communicate any concerns you might have with honesty.

If delayed ejaculation is just an occasional problem, then is important to keep in mind that for men and women, it won't always be possible to reach orgasm whenever they want to and that there is no shame in that fact. Sexual activity shouldn't focus solely on climaxing, after all.

How to improve delayed or inhibited ejaculation?

At the moment, there is no instant cure known for inhibited or delayed ejaculation. There are no drugs available that will help men achieve orgasm quicker, although there are some that are currently being tested.

However, since the vast majority of the time, the cause for delayed ejaculation is psychological, the best solution is to seek counseling.

The main objective of the therapy is to reduce a man's anxiety about giving up control so that he can achieve an orgasm during sexual intercourse without any significant difficulty. Many therapists will help the man relax and give him techniques to do so when he is with his partner.

If the cause for delayed ejaculation is the man's masturbation habits, then it is crucial to make some serious adjustments. While it is rarely required for the man to altogether quit masturbating, it is important to take a closer look at what might be causing the issue; for instance, if it is excessive porn use, then it might be necessary to find ways how to block adult sites if it has become an addiction. Some men aren't able to reach orgasm with anything but watching adult videos.

Some men might need to change their masturbation technique. The way they stroke their penis and stimulate it to achieve orgasm might be very different from the motion used during sexual intercourse. If such is the case, then the best course of action is to change the technique to something that more closely simulates the stroke performed during sex.

CHAPTER 13: ALL ABOUT CIRCUMCISION AND FORESKIN

Few topics can spark as much controversy and debate as circumcision. For a lot of families, the decision to circumcise their babies is pretty easy, because there are religious reasons that make is an obvious choice, but for other families, it can be a tricky decision.

It can be tough to have an educated conversation about circumcision because there are lots of differing opinions on the subject. Parents and men that have undergone the procedure tend to be heavily biased towards it. On the other hand, males that aren't circumcised tend to think very negatively about the procedure.

What is circumcision, and how is it usually done?

Circumcision is the surgical removal of the foreskin (the tissue that covers the glans of the penis). When the newborn baby is still in the hospital, the procedure is usually done using local anesthetic by a physician. In some cases, the parents may choose to have it done later, by a doctor that specializes in the male reproductive system.

It is a very ancient practice that was done in religious rites. Nowadays, it is still done as a rite in some religions. However, most parents nowadays choose to have their babies circumcised for other reasons other than religious.

The American Academy of Pediatrics agrees that circumcision can have certain benefits, but doesn't recommend it in every single case, and prefers to leave the decision to the baby's parents.

The benefits of circumcision

According to some experts, circumcision might reduce the risk of contracting HIV by a whopping 60% percent, and also reduce the risk of transmitting other STDs like HPV to their partners. There is also some evidence that the procedure might be able to help reduce the risk of penis cancer. It can also help prevent balanitis, an inflammation of the flans and balanoposthitis, an inflammation of the foreskin and glans.

It is very common for young boys and baby to suffer frequently from infant urinary tract infections, and circumcision helps reduce the risk of contracting these infections.

Some boys and men have a condition called phimosis, where they are unable to retract their foreskin, or they have paraphimosis, which is the inability to return their foreskin to its previous location.

Circumcision might also help keep the penis cleaner.

What are the risks of circumcision?

The risks of this procedure tend to be very low, as long as it is performed in a clean, sterile environment by a professional. Some of the typical minor complications tend to be minor bleeding and inflammation; however, more severe complications may occur in some cases. If the foreskin is cut too short, it may cause problems later on.

For adult males, some argue that circumcision tends to affect sexual satisfaction. Once the foreskin has been cut off, the penis, particularly the glans, tends to be less sensitive to touch. However, this point could be argued either way depending on each case, as some men have difficulty with ejaculation control, and having a slightly less sensitive glans would help them.

In some parts of the world, such as Europe, pediatricians don't usually recommend performing circumcision, not because it may have consequences or side effects, but mainly because they believe that there isn't enough evidence of the medical benefits of this procedure. They only recommend male circumcision where the child would definitively benefit from it. For instance, if the child has larger than normal foreskin, which may cause phimosis or paraphimosis later on.

Some critics of circumcision tend to think that it's unethical to cut the foreskin off without consent. The question they ask is: why expose a child to the risks of surgery for minimal medical benefit?

Adults and circumcision

A lot of experts mention that circumcision is easier when done in newborns than in adults.

When a newborn baby is circumcised, the procedure tends to be relatively simple. If the baby is around 12 pounds, the surgery is done by using local anesthesia. It becomes slightly more complicated afterward.

Adults that undergo the procedure often have to be put under general anesthesia. Another issue for a lot of people is insurance. Typically circumcision is not covered after the first 30 days of life. It may cost several hundred or thousands of dollars to get the procedure done as an adult.

Missing your foreskin

Some adults might be grateful that their parents chose to have the procedure done while they were newborn babies. Others, they might be wondering why their parents decided to go for the surgery without any apparent medical reason.

In previous decades, most sexual related subjects were considered taboo, and because of this, most men didn't speak up about circumcision and their opinions of it. Nowadays, such topics are much more commonplace, and because of this, we hear much more discussion about this controversial procedure.

Some years ago, uncircumcised males living in regions where the practice tends to be the norm, and not the exception often felt ashamed of the fact. Nowadays, in those regions, it is much more normal to accept the fact that you are uncircumcised as not opting for this option has become more typical.

If you are one of those adults that wonder why they didn't have a say in the matter, it is possible to restore your foreskin if you wish to do so. Some adult men argue that because the foreskin has around 100,000 nerve endings, there is a lot of enjoyment that they're not getting during masturbation and sex.

For some, this is enough for them to feel disappointed at the fact that they're missing this part of their penis.

You might choose to want to restore your foreskin for aesthetic reasons too. Aesthetically speaking, whether having foreskin looks better is entirely subjective and totally up to each individual's preferences. Men and women that see the circumcised penis as the norm will probably think they look better than uncircumcised penises and the opposite applies.

Restoring the foreskin

It is possible to restore the foreskin. Just as with male enhancement, the practice isn't new. It can be traced back thousands of years ago, as ancient civilizations such as the Greeks and Romans thought that exposure of the glans was improper.

And also, just as with male enhancement, there is the option of having surgery done.

However, growing the foreskin can be simpler than increasing your penis in length or thickness, and there are lots of cases of success without having to resort to the scalpel.

The nonsurgical methods rely on stretching the penis skin over a while until it eventually becomes permanently extended enough to cover the glans. The penis skin adapts and grows from the stress through tissue expansion. Surgical methods may graft the skin from other parts of the body to create something that looks very much like natural foreskin.

Another option is to buy devices that help expand the foreskin tissue. There are several different types of foreskin expansion devices.

Some of the most popular include TLC tuggers, where a silicone plug is placed against the glans, and then the shaft skin of the penis (that will eventually become the foreskin through tissue expansion) is pulled up and locked in place with a rubber cap. Other ball-shaped devices require you to draw over the penis skin or foreskin over it and then tape it into place.

If you are interested in growing your foreskin, we recommend trying out manual exercises before considering devices or surgery. As always, consult with your physician before trying any devices or manual exercises that might affect your health.

Manual exercise for foreskin regrowth

The most basic exercise for regrowing foreskin is manual tugging. In this exercise, you use tension generated by your hands to stretch the skin on your penis.

The stretching will promote tissue growth through mitosis.

The steps to perform this exercise are:

1.   Warm-up your penis just like you do at the beginning of the male enhancement routines, putting particular emphasis on the shaft of the penis with the warm water.

2.   Do 30-40 Kegels. Kegels will be useful for later, as it will help your erections become stronger by sending more blood in the penis.

3.   Grip the skin firmly at the base of the penis by using an OK sign (similar to the one used in the jelq exercise). Then slide the OK sign along the shaft and never release the grip you had on the skin area you were holding at the beginning. Do this until you start feeling the skin stretching significantly.

Try to keep this position no longer for as long you can maintain your erection or a maximum of 10 seconds. Whichever happens first.

4.   Try to shoot for at least 10 minutes a day. Try to stretch the penis skin slightly more during the last 3 to 5 repetitions and try to pull it towards the tip of your penis as hard as you can. Remember that pain is not ok. If you feel the signs of overtraining (discomfort, itchiness, pain, etc.), then this is your cue to decrease the intensity or frequency of the training sessions.

5.   This exercise can usually be done up to 6 days per week, but it depends on your ability to recover and how intense you are exercising. It takes a little time (some report two weeks) to start to see new skin developing.

Possible risks and side effects

Just as with male enhancement exercises, manual foreskin regrowth techniques are generally safe when practiced safely. The same applies to the use of devices. If you overtrain by performing the techniques too often or too intensely, you could easily damage the nerves in the skin through overstretching or rough treatment. If you stretch the skin tissue too far, it can also cause a lot of pain and damage.

Surgical procedures for foreskin restoration are usually more complicated and may result in skin loss, blood loss, infections, blood clots, and sepsis. If you're interested in such a procedure, it would be a good idea to talk to your doctor, as there might be some additional risks that are individual to you.

CHAPTER 14: Enhancing ejaculation

A lot of men will end their male enhancement journey once they reach their size goals, but some will also be interested in other types of "improvement." One of the most common concerns of men in the bedroom, besides penis size, is the amount of ejaculation volume.

Recent studies have confirmed that most men are not satisfied with the current size of their ejaculations. In some instances, this dissatisfaction might even cause high levels of anxiety that might affect their performance in bed.

This desire to have bigger loads probably comes from not almost limitless access to pornography.

Men that have continuously been exposed to these videos are used to seeing male pornstars that typically ejaculate enormous loads of semen when climaxing. Some of these male pornstars have admitted that there is no secret to their big loads and that they've always have been able to ejaculate large amounts of semen.

Interestingly enough, having a big load isn't common. According to research, the typical male ejaculates between three and five milliliters, or in other words, about a teaspoon of liquid. Also, it's important to be aware that the amount of semen that men produce varies with age. The peak years are between ages 30-35, and then it tends to decrease slowly.

If you are part of the men that are interested in increasing their ejaculation size, you might be wondering if there are things that you can do that can give you real results. Just as with the male enhancement industry, there are a lot of scams and frauds around.

There are lots of pills and supplements sold that promise to increase your load. However, not many of them work.

Have you ever asked yourself what semen is made out of? The answer might surprise you. Semen is mostly water, with lots of different proteins, vitamins, amino acids, and minerals. Only around 1% of semen is sperm.

Let's take a look at some of the things that have been proven to increase ejaculate volume.

The first recommendation might sound obvious, but it almost always works: wait three days between ejaculations. In 3 days, the body completely replenishes your semen reserves. Of course, waiting three days to ejaculate again can be impractical in some cases, but for those special occasions when you want to impress your partner, it won't hurt to wait.

Waiting beyond three days to have an even bigger load won't work, as it seems that there is no increase after that point.

Before looking at supplements, we would suggest specific lifestyle changes that will most likely give you a boost in ejaculation volume. Including more of the nutrients that the body uses for creating semen will significantly help you achieve bigger loads and also ejaculate more often if you wish to do so.

Because semen consists of vitamin B12, chlorine, calcium, zinc, sodium, lactic acid, magnesium, vitamin C, etc., then the logical conclusion would be to include more whole foods that contain plenty of these substances to help boost the size and quality of your loads. Some researchers support supplementing with Vitamin D to increase semen quality, even though semen contains no Vitamin D.

The first and most important recommendation that will have the most impact on the size and quality of your loads is making sure you are always well hydrated. Up to 60-70% of the human body is made out of water. Most organs in your body need water to function correctly. Because water is also the most significant component of semen, you are limiting the size of your loads by not being adequately hydrated. Make sure that you always have access to a bottle of water, even when you're not at home.

Losing weight is another health recommendation that improves a lot of different conditions. It is no wonder that losing weight (if you're currently overweight or obese) will also impact the quality of your loads. Over thirty percent of men who are obese have a lower than average sperm count. A shocking amount of obese men have an almost nonexistent sperm count. Losing weight if you are currently overweight is a guaranteed way to increase the size of your loads.

Because semen is partly constituted by antioxidants, the consumption of specific whole foods such as vegetables and fruits will cause a positive impact in your semen production. The veggies that tend to be most abundant in antioxidants are greens, and for fruits, it is berries the ones that are considered one of the richest sources.

One vegetable seems to be king among those that are looking to increase the size of their loads though: celery. A lot of people from pornstars to ordinary men seem to sing praises of this vegetable, and it's supposedly miraculous properties for increasing the size of one's load. Celery is very rich in vitamins A and C and minerals such as potassium and folate, components essential for the production of semen. Because of this, celery can significantly help increase the size of your loads. Because celery is almost none existant as a supplement and is extremely cheap, there has been little research done on whether it improves the quality of semen or not. However, it is probably the most recommended food by a lot of men for this specific purpose.

Zinc is an essential mineral for male health and semen production, and it can be found in foods such as eggs, meat, legumes, nuts, and seeds. Men that have low levels of this mineral tend to have low fertility problems, low libido, and decreased semen quality and quantity. Having enough zinc in one's diet is not complicated, as there are lots of foods that have proper amounts of this mineral.

Eating several portions of legumes or meat (depending on the type of diet you have) and a few handfuls of nuts every week should do the trick for most. But if you are still having issues getting enough zinc, there are lots of supplements available that can help you reach the daily recommended intake.

Exercise is also a good recommendation, but never go overboard. While moderate exercise, done regularly 3-6 times per week can increase your sperm count and load size, overtraining and doing severe high-intensity exercise will do the opposite.

The best types of exercise for increasing semen quantity are cardio and weight lifting. Cardio activities improve blood flow, while weight lifting can help with testosterone production.

Decreasing one's tobacco and alcohol consumption will also impact sperm production, which comes to no surprise to most people, as these two substances tend to affect most of our body's functions.

If you are currently taking lengthy baths with hot water, this might be affecting your sperm count and load quality. Prolonged exposure to heat near the testes damages sperm very quickly.

Getting enough sleep is also crucial for overall male health. Sleep helps our body recover and repair itself. If you are currently not sleeping enough, this will eventually take a toll on your body, and semen quality will decrease.

Depending on your levels of activity, anywhere from 7 to 9 hours should be enough sleep to replenish your body fully.

Some supplements available haven't yet been studied extensively regarding whether or not they have a significant impact on the quality of our semen. However, some men that have used them, in some cases have reported that they have made a big difference in the quality and size of their loads without having to do little else.

The first of these supplements is lecithin. Lecithin is composed of a combination of fatty acids that some believe improve semen quality. This substance also has been shown to enhance the quality of semen and the reproductive traits of some animals, such as in rabbits.

The U.S. food and drug administration has recognized this substance to be safe for human consumption.

There are little side effects known to be caused by Lecithin, and it should be safe to add to most diets after consulting with a medical advisor first.

L-arginine is another one of those seemingly miraculous substances that a lot of men swear by. Men take L-arginine primarily to boost their libido and stamina, but some have reported that it also works wonders for improving their erections. L-arginine seems to promote better blood circulation, which makes erections stronger and stiffer. Because of these benefits, it is a popular supplement with men in their 50's and beyond, but it can also be taken by those in their 20's and 30's if a boost in sexual performance is what they seek.

While it is not common to tale K-arginine exclusively to increase semen size, some men take L-arginine specifically for this purpose.

Ashwagandha is a very popular herb that can help in several different instances. The primary reason why people take this herb as a supplement is to decrease levels of stress (it may help balance out cortisol production). People that tend to be constantly stressed out typically have hormonal disbalances that may go from mild to severe, depending on the levels of stress they experience daily.

Butea Superba is a herb from Thailand that has been used to improve sexual health for a long time. Some people report that it may also help in some instances of erectile dysfunction. While it is not a herb that is normally taken for increasing semen quantity, for a lot of men it has helped precisely with that.

For men, having high levels of stress means that testosterone production can be affected. Ashwagandha is a herb that has been found to balance out cortisol in some people.

Men that have taken this herb report an improvement in their overall mood, sexual desire, stamina, and semen quantity.

Some of the exercises explained in this book are great for exercising the muscles that will help you shoot your load a further distance. While they don't help increase the size of your loads, they will help give the appearance of a bigger load through a stronger ejaculation. The best exercises for this purpose are edging and Kegels.

Finally, in some instances, smaller loads or a low sperm count can also be caused by hormonal disbalances. Not surprisingly, the number one hormonal cause for small loads is low testosterone. Low testosterone is a hormonal disbalance that affects a lot of men and can cause a lot of male sexual issues such as erectile dysfunction and low libido. If you suspect that you may have low testosterone levels, you can always check with your doctor with a blood test.

In some cases, the dr. will be able to recommend you hormone replacement therapy that will help you feel more energetic, focus better, and a host of male sexual benefits.

What about the taste?

A lot of curious men have wondered what their semen tastes like at one point. The answer might be anything from slightly sweet to salty or that it takes similar to detergent or even battery acid. Why is there such a significant disparity in taste from individual to individual?

The reason is straightforward: there are several factors that influence the taste and smell of semen. Body PH, diet, and individual habits are probably the factors that affect its taste the most. People that eat lots of junk food, drink little water and smoke and drink alcohol tend to have very bitter tasting semen.

The primary reason for wanting to change or improve the taste of your semen is to make oral sex more pleasurable for your partner. Some men find it very pleasurable when their partner swallows their load after climaxing. However, some people can have a very difficult time swallowing their partner's semen because they find the smell or taste of it very off-putting.

How our diet affects the taste of semen

Anything that we end up putting in our bodies, whether it's food or drugs such as tobacco or medicine, ends up affecting all of our bodily fluids and secretions not just in semen. Your sweat and saliva, for instance, are also affected by what you put in your body.

You might have heard of cases where a person has a powerful body odor and how they managed to control it via changes in their diet or lifestyle. Well, the same applies to semen and its taste.

Semen usually has a pH level higher than 7 and is alkaline. The reason for its alkalinity is to protect sperm inside the naturally acidic vagina. By protecting the sperm, it helps ensure reproductive success.

What makes semen taste bad?

The biggest offenders are the following:

-Excessive meat consumption: tends to make semen too salty and sometimes extra bitter.

-Excessive caffeine consumption: just as with meat, having too much of it can result in a bitter taste.

-Medicine: Some medications can make all of your body fluids smell, and taste worse.

-Asparagus: you've probably noticed how strong your pee smells after consuming too much of it. It doesn't do the taste or smell of semen any favors also.

-Junk food: Most junk food has chemicals in it that make semen taste worse.

If you want to make your semen taste as best as possible, it is a good idea to limit the consumption of the above as much as you can (whenever possible of course). It is not bad to indulge occasionally, like in the case of caffeine and alcohol, but consistent consumption will inevitably end up affecting your semen's taste negatively.

What makes semen taste good?

On the other hand, here's what usually helps semen taste better:

-Water: Drinking enough water will not only improve the size of your ejaculation but its taste too.

-Celery: this also helps improve both the volume and taste of semen, as it includes a lot of the vitamins and minerals that the body uses to produce it.

-Spices and herbs: the best ones for sweetening up your semen's taste are cinnamon, peppermint, parsley, and wheatgrass

-Fruits: a lot of fruits have a positive impact on semen taste. You have probably heard about pineapple before, but some other good ones are cranberries, blueberries, kiwi fruits, and plumbs.

The next time you're engaged in oral sex with your partner, ask them how your semen tastes.

Try to make adjustments to your eating habits until you arrive at a point where your partner is delighted with its taste and smell. You probably won't have to make too many adjustments to get there, and your reward will probably be more frequent and more satisfying oral sex sessions.